One-Word Substitution

One-Word Substitution

Pallavi Borgohain

Published by
PRABHAT PRAKASHAN PVT. LTD.
4/19 Asaf Ali Road,
New Delhi-110 002 (INDIA)
e-mail: prabhatbooks@gmail.com

ISBN 978-93-5048-182-0
ONE-WORD SUBSTITUTION
by Pallavi Borgohain

Edition
2025

Price
₹ 300.00 (Rupees Three Hundred only)

Printed at
Narula Printers, Delhi

Introduction

Writing is basically an open-ended medium of expression used for conveying ideas and feelings to others. In a way, it is used with an intention to make a communication long lasting and of course it is used as a succinct means to express thoughts, now as well as for future.

However as an art form, writing needs motivation and appropriate vocabulary. Also, enough attribution is required to make the writings spicy, so that it is easily intelligible to the readers.

Whether you are a professional or a student, you should have a good vocabulary through which you can clearly communicate your ideas. You should be well aware of your readers and use vocabulary accordingly. Therefore, it is worthwhile to constantly work at improving your knowledge of words.

The good knowledge of one-word substitutes is necessary for enhancing your vocabulary skills. While writing a paragraph, a report or an essay, you should always try to use those words that represent exactly the same meaning you want to convey. One should avoid using phrases and making the writings unnecessarily long. A precise writing is always loved by the readers.

Skillful writing is not easy; it is slightly tricky and involves great mastery and appropriate use of vocabulary. Often overused words and repetitions spoil the charm of writing. That is why it is necessary to balance the writings with one-word substitutes and appropriate words.

—Pallavi Borgohain

Contents

1

Often Used One-Word Substitutes

One-word substitutes are a great boon for effective writing. A precise writing is appreciated by all. One-word substitutes help the speaker or writer to express his thoughts and ideas precisely. There are some common one-word substitutes which are used daily. Here is a list of often-used one-word substitutes which will help you to enrich your word store.

Let us refresh our memory and identify some one-word substitutes for a phrase or a clause, which we normally used in our life day in and out.

1. A partner in crime – accomplice
2. A masculine woman – amazon
3. A person who can use both hands with the same skill – ambis-dextrous
4. A place of permanent residence – domicile
5. One who is not a professional – amateur
6. To turn friends into enemies – alienate
7. An insect with many legs – centipede
8. A man whose manners are like women rather than men – effeminate
9. A disease peculiar to a country – endemic
10. A state of extreme joy – ecstasy

11. One vowed to a single life – celibate
12. One who lives for a hundred years or even more – centenarian
13. A person who regards the whole world as his home and is free from regional prejudices – cosmopolitan
14. One who leaves his native place to settle in another – emigrant
15. One who comes to a foreign land to settle there – immigrant
16. One who is not easily pleased – fastidious
17. To injure a man's reputation by slanderous words – defame
18. Having peculiar habit – idiosyncrasy
19. That which has always existed and will exist – eternal
20. Words inscribed on a tomb – epitaph

□

2

Common One-Word Substitutes Used In Various Fields

One-Word Substitutes Related To General Science

General Science is an important subject that we all must have studied. Here are some one-word substitutes related to science.

1. A study of the body – Physiology
2. A study of animal – Zoology
3. A study of birds – Ornithology
4. A study of ancient things – Archaeology
5. A study of man – Anthropology
6. A study of races – Ethnology
7. A study of derivation of words – Etymology
8. The science of origin and growth of language – Philology
9. The science of human mind – Psychology
10. The science which deals with the investigation of ultimate reality – Philosophy
11. The science of articulate sounds – Phonetics
12. The science of the earth's crust, its composition, structure and history of its development – Geology
13. The science which deals with the state and its government – Politics

14. The science of valid thinking – Logic
15. The science of the evolution and classification of human society – Sociology
16. The science of magnitude whether linear, or superficial or solid with their properties and relations and space – Geometry
17. The science of internal structure of metals – Metallography
18. The science of wealth – Economics
19. The science of bodily structure – Anatomy
20. The science of teaching – Pedagogy

One-Word Substitutes Related To Human Traits

Various human traits and attributes can be described in one-word. Here are some one-word substitutes representing human character.

1. One who is greedy for money – avaricious
2. One who is a newcomer – neophyte
3. One who is out to subvert a government – anarchist
4. One who is recovering from illness – convalescent
5. One who is all powerful – omnipotent
6. One who is present everywhere – omnipresent
7. One who knows everything – omniscient
8. One who is easily deceived – gullible
9. One who does not make mistakes – infallible
10. One who can do anything for money – mercenary
11. One who has no money – pauper
12. One who changes sides – turncoat
13. One who works for free – volunteer
14. One who loves books – bibliophile
15. One who can speak two languages – bilingual
16. One who donates for charitable purpose – philanthropist

17. One who dislikes mankind – misanthrope
18. One who looks on the bright side of things – optimist
19. One who looks on the dark side of things – pessimist
20. One who doubts the existence of God – agnostic
21. One who pretends to be what he is not – hypocrite
22. One incapable of being tired – indefatigable
23. One who helps others – good samaritan
24. One who copies from other writers – plagiarist
25. One who hates women – misogynist
26. One who knows many languages – polyglot
27. One who is fond of sensuous pleasures – epicure
28. One who thinks only of himself – egoist
29. One who thinks only of welfare of women – feminist
30. One who is indifferent to pleasure or pain – stoic
31. One who is quite like a woman – effeminate
32. One who has strange habits – eccentric
33. One who speaks less – reticent
34. One who goes on foot – pedestrian
35. One who dies without a will – intestate
36. One who always thinks himself to be ill – valetudinarian
37. One who can throw his voice – ventriloquist
38. One who doesn't know how to read and write – illiterate
39. One who damages public property – vandal
40. One who does something not professionally but for pleasure – amateur
41. One who does not believe in the existence of God – atheist
42. One who has narrow and prejudiced views – bigot
43. A man who has too much enthusiasm for his own religion – fanatic
44. One who thinks only for oneself, a person who is selfish, self absorbed and self centered – egoist

45. One who feels sympathetic towards human beings – humanitarian
46. A person who remains unmoved and unaffected by other people's opinions, arguments or suggestions – impervious
47. One who is unable to pay his debts – insolvent
48. A person who does not believe in the institution of marriage – misogamist
49. Somebody who works or serves only for personal profit. Also, a professional soldier paid to fight for an army other than that of his or her country – mercenary
50. One who does not care for art, literature etc. – philistine

One-Word Substitutes Related To Political Science

Politics has a big role to play in our day-to-day life. Here are one-word substitutes that are related to politics and the study of political science.

1. Acracy : government by none; anarchy
2. Adhocracy : government in an unstructured fashion; an unstructured organization
3. Albocracy : government by white people
4. Anarchy : government by none
5. Androcracy : government by men
6. Anemocracy : government by the wind or by whim
7. Angelocracy : government by angels
8. Antarchy : opposition to government; anarchy
9. Argentocracy : government by money
10. Aristarchy : government by the best
11. Arithmocracy : government by simple majority
12. Autarchy : government by an absolute ruler

13. Autocracy : government by one individual
14. Barbarocracy : government by barbarians
15. Beerocracy : government by brewers or brewing interests
16. Bestiocracy : rule by beasts
17. Biarchy : government ruled by two people
18. Bureaucracy : government by civil servants
19. Cannonarchy : government by superior firepower or by cannons
20. Capelocracy : government by shopkeepers
21. Chiliarchy : government by one thousand people
22. Chirocracy : government by physical force
23. Chromatocracy : government by rulers of a particular skin colour
24. Chrysoaristocracy : government by the wealthy; plutocracy
25. Chrysocracy : government by the wealthy; plutocracy
26. Corpocracy : government by corporate bureaucrats
27. Cosmarchy : rulership over the entire world, esp. by the devil
28. Cottonocracy : government by those involved in the cotton trade
29. Cryptarchy : secret rulership
30. Decarchy : government controlled by ten individuals decarchy
31. Demarchy : government by the people; popular government
32. Democracy : government by the people
33. Demonarchy : government by a demon

34. Demonocracy : government by demons or evil forces
35. Despotocracy : government by despots or tyrants
36. Diabolocracy : government by the devil
37. Dodecarchy : government by twelve people
38. Doulocracy : government by slaves
39. Dulocracy : government by slaves; doulocracy
40. Dyarchy : government by two people; diarchy
41. Ecclesiarchy : government by clerics or ecclesiastical authorities
42. Endarchy : centralised government
43. Ergatocracy : government by the workers or the working class
44. Ethnarchy : government over an ethnic group
45. Ehnocracy : government by an ethnic group or race
46. Exarchy : government by bishops
47. Foolocracy : government by fools
48. Gerontocracy : government by the aged
49. Gunarchy : government by women; gynarchy
50. Gymnasiarchy : government over a school or academy
51. Gynaecocracy : government by women; gynarchy
52. Gynocracy : government by women; gynarchy
53. Hagiarchy : government by saints or holy persons
54. Hagiocracy : government by holy men
55. Hamarchy : government by a cooperative body of parts
56. Hecatontarchy : government by one hundred people
57. Hendecarchy : government by eleven people
58. Heptarchy : government by seven people

59. Heroarchy : government by heroes
60. Hetaerocracy : government by paramours
61. Heterarchy : government by a foreign ruler
62. Hierarchy : government by a ranked body; government by priests
63. Hierocracy : government by priests or religious ministers
64. Hipparchy : rule or control of horses
65. Hoplarchy : government by the military
66. Hyperanarchy : condition of extreme anarchy
67. Hyperarchy : excessive government
68. Iatrarchy : government by physicians
69. Idiocracy : personal rule; self-rule
70. Infantocracy : government by an infant
71. Isocracy : equal political power
72. Jesuitocracy : government by Jesuits
73. Juntocracy : government by a junta
74. Kakistocracy : government by the worst
75. Kleptocracy : government by thieves
76. Kritarchy : government by judges
77. Landocracy : government by the propertied class; timocracy
78. Logocracy : government of words
79. Matriarchy : government by women or mothers
80. Meritocracy : government by the meritorious
81. Merocracy : government by a part of the citizenry
82. Mesocracy : government by the middle classes
83. Metrocracy : government by mothers or women; matriarchy
84. Millionocracy : government by millionaires
85. Millocracy : government by mill owners

86. Mobocracy : government by mobs or crowds
87. Moneyocracy : government by the monied classes
88. Monocracy : government by one individual
89. Myriarchy : government by ten thousand individuals
90. Narcokleptocracy : government by those who profit from trade in illegal drugs
91. Navarchy : rulership over the seas
92. Neocracy : government by new or inexperienced rulers
93. Nomocracy : government based on legal system; rule of law
94. Ochlocracy : government by mobs
95. Octarchy : government by eight people
96. Oligarchy : government by a few
97. Paedarchy : government by children
98. Panarchy : universal rule or dominion
99. Pantarchy : government by all the people; world government
100. Pantisocracy : government by all equally
101. Paparchy : government by the pope
102. Papyrocracy : government by newspapers or literature
103. Parsonarchy : government by parsons
104. Partocracy : government by a single unopposed political party
105. Patriarchy : government by men or fathers
106. Pedantocracy : government by pedants or strict rule bound scholars
107. Pentarchy : government by five individuals
108. Phallocracy : government by men
109. Philosophocracy : government by philosophers

110. Phylarchy : government by a specific class or tribe
111. Physiocracy : government according to natural laws or principles
112. Pigmentocracy : government by those of one skin colour
113. Plantocracy : government by plantation owners
114. Plousiocracy : government by the wealthy; plutocracy
115. Plutarchy : government by the wealthy; plutocracy
116. Plutocracy : government by the wealthy
117. Polarchy : government by many people; polyarchy
118. Policeocracy : government by police
119. Pollarchy : government by the multitude or a mob; ochlocracy
120. Polyarchy : government by many people
121. Polycracy : government by many rulers; polyarchy
122. Popocracy : government by populists
123. Pornocracy : government by harlots
124. Prophetocracy : government by a prophet
125. Psephocracy : government resulting from election by ballot
126. Ptochocracy : government by beggars or paupers; wholesale pauperization
127. Punditocracy : government by political pundits
128. Quangocracy : rule of quasi-autonomous non-governmental organizations
129. Rotocracy : government by those who control rotten boroughs

130. Septarchy : government by seven rulers; heptarchy
131. Shopocracy : government by shopkeepers
132. Slavocracy : government by slave-owners
133. Snobocracy : government by snobs
134. Sociocracy : government by society as a whole
135. Squarsonocracy : government by landholding clergymen
136. Squatterarchy : government by squatters; squattocracy
137. Squattocracy : government by squatters
138. Squirearchy : government by squires
139. Squirocracy : government by squires; squirearchy
140. Statocracy : government by the state alone, without ecclesiastical influence
141. Stratarchy : rulership over an army
142. Stratocracy : military rule or despotism
143. Strumpetocracy : government by strumpets
144. Synarchy : joint sovereignty
145. Technocracy : government by technical experts
146. Tetradarchy : government by four people; tetrarchy
147. Tetrarchy : government by four people
148. Thalassiarchy : sovereignty of the seas; thalassocracy
149. Thalassocracy : sovereignty of the seas
150. Thearchy : rule by a god or gods; body of divine rulers
151. Theatrocracy : goverment by gathered assemblies of citizens
152. Theocracy : government by priests or by religious law

153.	Timarchy	: government by the propertied class; timocracy
154.	Timocracy	: government by the propertied class
155.	Tritarchy	: government by three people; triarchy
156.	Tritheocracy	: government by three gods
157.	Whiggarchy	: government by Whigs
158.	Xenocracy	: government by a body of foreigners
159.	Hung	: Assembly or parliament in which no party has got clear majority
160.	Ambassador	: A diplomatic minister of the higher order sent by a country to another

□

3

One-Word For A Group Of Words

The words that a person uses to express himself tell more about him than he thinks. One word substitutes play a very important role in conversation because through them a person can speak and write precisely. Often people write and speak garrulously using many flowery words. The listener may not have enough time to listen to such long conversations. Sometimes they do not understand what the speaker is saying. This is because the conversation loses its connectivity due to its lengthy nature. But precise words are easily understood.

It is good to be verbose but sometimes verbosity leads to boredom. Therefore, to converse and write precisely, it is necessary to have a good knowledge about one-word substitutes.

In English, there are many single words for a group of words or phrases. Learn these words and avoid the fear of being unintelligible while speaking and writing.

1. Abolish : do away completely.
2. Abbreviation : the shortened form of a word or phrase.
3. Accelerate : to increase the speed; to hasten the progress

4. Actuary : a person who calculates premium.
5. Aggravate : to increase the gravity of an offence or the intensity of a disease.
6. Alienate : to make enemy of friends.
7. Amphibian : a kind of animal that lives on both land and water and basically breeds in water.
8. Aristocracy : people of noble families or the highest social class. (Aristocracy is also a form of the government where a small group of people, especially hereditary nobility rules the country.)
9. Cannibal : someone who eats human flesh.
10. Diplomat/Envoy : a diplomatic minister of the higher order sent by a country to another.
11. Ambiguous : statements open to more than one interpretation or of uncertain nature.
12. Ambivalent : uncertain or unable to decide
13. Amnesty : to grant general pardon
14. Anonymous : a letter, poem etc., whose author is unknown.
15. Anarchy : absence of government
16. Answerable : a person liable to be called to account for his action.

17. Appreciate : to rise in value: be grateful
18. Auditor : one who makes an official examination of accounts.
19. Autobiography : the life story of a man written by himself.
20. Biography : life story of a man written by others.
21. Bureaucracy : a form of government ruled by the officials.
22. Bourgeois : a member of the middle class.
23. Colleagues : people working together in the same office or department.
24. Congenital : belonging or pertaining to an individual from birth.
25. Contemporary : occurring in the same period of time.
26. Credulous : a person who believes easily whatever he is told.
27. Depreciate : to go down in value.
28. Disenfranchisement : the act of withdrawing certification or terminating a franchise.
29. Delegate : to give authority or task to another.
30. Drawn/Tie : A game or batter in which neither party wins.
31. Edible : Something which is fit to be eaten.

32.	Elucidate	:	To explain something mysterious or difficult: to make clear.
33.	Emphasize	:	To lay special stress on.
34.	Equilibrium	:	A state of perfect balance.
35.	Eradicate	:	To root out an evil, disease.
36.	Extempore or Impromptu	:	A speech delivered without any previous preparation.
37.	Embezzlement	:	inappropriate expenditure or misappropriation of money
38.	Facsimile	:	an exact copy.
39.	Fastidious	:	someone who is not easily pleased.
40.	Germicide	:	a medicine used to kill germs
41.	Honorary	:	work for which no salary is given.
42.	Illegible	:	that which cannot be read.
43.	Illicit	:	that is prohibited by law.
44.	Inaudible	:	a sound that cannot be heard.
45.	Incomprehensible	:	a statement which cannot be understood.
46.	Incorrigible	:	one who cannot be corrected.
47.	Inexplicable	:	that which cannot be explained.
48.	Infallible	:	incapable of failure or error.
49.	Illiterate	:	a person who cannot read or write.
50.	Infanticide	:	the killing of an infant.
51.	Inflammable	:	something that catches fire quickly and easily.
52.	Inimitable	:	some kind of method that cannot be imitated.

53. Insatiable : that which cannot be satisfied.

54. Invulnerable : that which cannot be hurt.

55. Introspection : to contemplate on one's own thoughts and conduct.

56. Invisible : a thing that cannot be seen.

57. Irrevocable : something which cannot be retracted or withdrawn.

58. Jurisdiction : the area over which an official has control.

59. Maiden : the first speech made by a person.

60. Numismatics : collection and study of coins or medals.

61. Omnivorous : an animal or a human being that eats any kind of food.

62. Potable : water fit for drinking.

63. Psephology : systematic study of election trends.

64. Soporific : a drug or other substance that induces sleep.

65. Sinecure : an office with minimal duties.

□

One-Word Related To Different Types Of Killings

Human beings have an unwarranted tendency for killing things. Because of the inordinate tendency to kill they have also developed certain one-word terms to describe various types of killings. Almost all words related to killings end in the suffix 'cide', which is derived from the Latin word *caedere,* meaning 'to kill'.

1. Aborticide : killing of a fetus; abortion
2. Amicicide : murder of a friend
3. Avicide : killing of birds, birdicide
4. Bacillicide : killer of bacteria
5. Biocide : killing living material
6. Bovicide : slaughter of cattle; one who kills cattle
7. Ceticide : killing of whales and other cetaceans
8. Cimicide : substance used to kill bed-bugs
9. Ecocide : destruction of the environment
10. Episcopicide : killing of bishops
11. Famicide : one who destroys another's reputation; slanderer
12. Felicide : killing of a cat

13. Femicide : killing of a woman
14. Filicide : killing of one's own child
15. Floricide : killing or killer of flowers
16. Foeticide : killing a fetus
17. Formicide : substance that kills ants
18. Fratricide : killing of one's brother
19. Fungicide : killing of fungus
20. Genocide : killing of a race or ethnic group
21. Germicide : substance that kills germs
22. Giganticide : killing of a giant
23. Gynaecide : killing of women
24. Herbicide : killing of plants
25. Hereticide : killing of heretics
26. Homicide : killing of a human being
27. Infanticide : killing of an infant
28. Insecticide : killing of insects
29. Larvicide : killing of larvae
30. Liberticide : destruction of liberty
31. Lupicide : killing of a wolf
32. Mariticide : killing or killer of one's husband
33. Menticide : reduction of mind by psychological pressure
34. Microbicide : killing or killer of microbes
35. Miticide : agent which kills mites
36. Molluscicide : killing of mollusks
37. Muscicide : substance for killing flies
38. Neonaticide : killing or killer of a newborn infant
39. Ovicide : killing the eggs of insects
40. Parasiticide : killing of parasites
41. Parenticide : killing or killer of one's parents

42. Parricide	:	killing of parents or a parent-like close relative
43. Patricide	:	killing of one's father
44. Perdricide	:	killer of partridges
45. Pesticide	:	killing of pests
46. Prolicide	:	killing of offspring; killing of the human race
47. Pulicide	:	flea-killer
48. Raticide	:	substance or person who kills rats
49. Regicide	:	killing of a monarch
50. Rodenticide	:	killing of rodents
51. Senicide	:	killing of old men
52. Serpenticide	:	killing or killer of a snake
53. Siblicide	:	killing or killer of a sibling
54. Silvicide	:	substance that kills trees
55. Sororicide	:	killing of one's own sister
56. Speciocide	:	destruction of an entire species
57. Spermicide	:	killing of sperm
58. Sporicide	:	killing of spores
59. Suicide	:	killing of oneself
60. Taeniacide	:	killing of tapeworms
61. Tauricide	:	killing or killer of a bull
62. Trypanocide	:	killing of trypanosomes
63. Tyrannicide	:	killing or killer of a tyrant
64. Urbicide	:	destruction of a city
65. Ursicide	:	killing or killer of a bear
66. Utricide	:	one who stabs an inflated skin vessel instead of killing someone
67. Uxoricide	:	killing of one's own wife
68. Vaticide	:	killing or killer of a prophet
69. Verbicide	:	destroying the meaning of a word
70. Vermicide	:	killing of worms

71. Vespacide : substance or person who kills wasps
72. Viricide : killing of viruses; killing of men or of husbands
73. Virucide : killing of viruses
74. Vulpicide : killing of a fox
75. Weedicide : something that kills weeds

□

Uncommon One-Word Substitutes

There are various uncommon one-word substitutes. They are very rarely used in day-to-day conversation. However it is quite interesting to know about these one-word substitutes used in various fields. Know more about these one-word substitutes used in various fields.

One-Word substitute Used In Literature:

From ancient times there are a wide range of literary terms used as one-word substitutes for various things associated to literature. Here are some of them:

1. Acronym : a word formed from initial letters of another word
2. Allonym : the name taken by an author from another person.
3. Antonym : a word whose meaning is the opposite of a given word
4. Autonym : a writer's real name; work published under writer's own name
5. Caconym : wrongly derived name
6. Cohyponym : word which is one of multiple hyponyms of another word

7. Exonym : name for a town or country in a foreign language
8. Heteronym : words having same spelling but different sound and meaning
9. Homonym : words having the same sound but different meanings
10. Hypernym : word representing a class of words or things
11. Isonym : word having the same derivation or form as another
12. Meronym : word whose relation to another is a part to the whole
13. Metronymy : to name after the mother's or female line
14. Paedonymic : name taken from one's child
15. Paranym : Word whose meaning altered to conceal evasion
16. Paronym : word from same root or having same sound as another
17. Patronym : name derived from father's name
18. Polyonym : name consisting of several words
19. Pseudonym : fictitious name used by an author
20. Retronym : new name as modification of older term used alone
21. Synonym : word whose meaning is the same as another word
22. Tautonym : taxonomic name in which genus and species are the same
23. Teknonymy : the naming of the parent from the child
24. Toponym : place name derived from geographical feature
25. Trionym : name consisting of three words

One-Words Related To Different Forms Of Worship

Diffferent forms of worship have different names. People often practice crazy forms of worshipping. Some of the one word substitutes referring to various forms for worship are listed below. The words ends in suffix "-latry", adopted from the e Greek word *latreuein*, which means to worship.

1. Aischrolatry : the practice of worshipping filth, dirt, or smut
2. Allotheism : belief in or worship of strange gods
3. Angelolatry : the practice of worshipping angels
4. Anthropolatry : the practice of worshipping human beings
5. Arborolatry : the practice of worshipping trees
6. Archaeolatry : the practice of worshipping archaic things or old customs
7. Astrolatry : the practice of worshipping stars
8. Bardolatry : the practice of worshipping Shakespeare
9. Bibliolatry : the practice of worshipping the bible or other books
10. Christolatry : the practice of worshipping Christ
11. Cosmolatry : the practice of worshipping the world
12. Cynolatry : the practice of worshipping dogs
13. Demonolatry : the practice of worshipping demons
14. Ecclesiolatry : to have excessive devotion to Church tradition and form
15. Epeolatry : the practice of worshipping words

16. Episcopolatry : the practice of worshipping bishops
17. Gamidolatry : the practice of worshippin-gmarriage
18. Gastrolatry : excessive love of food, gluttony
19. Geolatry : earth-worship
20. Grammatolatry : the worship of letters and words
21. Gyniolatry : having deep respect or devotion for women
22. Hagiolatry : the worship or reverence for saints
23. Heliolatry : worship of the Sun
24. Hierolatry : worship of saints or sacred things
25. Hygeiolatry : excessive devotion to health
26. Ichthyolatry : the worship of fish
27. Iconolatry : image-worship
28. Ideolatry : worship of ideas
29. Idiolatry : self-worship; egotism
30. Ignicolist : someone who worships fire.
31. Litholatry : the practice of worshipping stone
32. Lordolatry : the practice of worshipping nobility
33. Mariolatry : the practice of worshipping virgin mother
34. Martyrolatry : excessive devotion to martyrs
35. Mechanolatry : the worship of machines
36. Monolatry : to worship of one god without excluding belief in others
37. Necrolatry : the practice of worshipping the dead
38. Neolatry : the practice of worshipping novelty

39. Onolatry : the practice of worshipping asses or donkeys
40. Ophiolatry : worship of snakes
41. Pandemonism : worship of spirits dwelling in all forms of nature
42. Patriolatry : to have excessive devotion or worship of one's native country
43. Physiolatry : nature-worship
44. Planetolatry : worship of the planets
45. Plutolatry : worship of wealth
46. Poetolatry : worship of poets
47. Pseudolatry : false worship
48. Pyrolatry : fire-worship
49. Selenolatry : worship of the moon
50. Statolatry : worship of the state
51. Staurolatry : worship of the cross or crucifix
52. Symbolatry : undue worship of symbols
53. Thaumatolatry : worship of miracles or wonders
54. Theriolatry : animal-worship
55. Zoolatry : devotion to animals or pets

One-Words Used To Define Different Forms Of Art

Some one-word substitutes associated with some uncommon arts are mentioned below.

1. Agonistics : art and theory of prize-fighting
2. Anaglyptics : art of carving in bas-relief
3. Castrametation : the art of designing a camp
4. Catechectics : the art of teaching by question and answer
5. Chalcotriptics : art of taking rubbings from ornamental brasses

6.	Ciselure	:	the art of chasing metal
7.	Diagraphics	:	art of making diagrams or drawings
8.	Dramaturgy	:	art of producing and staging dramatic works
9.	Homiletics	:	the art of preaching
10.	Lexigraphy	:	art of definition of words
11.	Magirics	:	art of cookery
12.	Magnanerie	:	art of raising silkworms
13.	Manège	:	the art of horsemanship
14.	Nautics	:	art of navigation
15.	Paedotrophy	:	art of rearing children
16.	Psalligraphy	:	the art of paper-cutting to make pictures
17.	Pseudology	:	art or science of lying
18.	Schematonics	:	art of using gesture to express tones
19.	Sciagraphy	:	art of shading
20.	Siderography	:	art of engraving on steel
21.	Stratography	:	art of leading an army
22.	Taxidermy	:	art of curing and stuffing animals
23.	Turnery	:	art of turning in a lathe
24.	Typography	:	the art of printing or using type
25.	Xylography	:	the art of engraving on wood

Rare Love Words

The one-words related to love and attraction ends in the suffix philia. The suffix phils is adopted from the greek word Greek *phileein* which means to love, and so a 'philia' is a special love, affection, attraction or preference for a certain type of thing. The list highlights some of the unique one-words substitutes associated with love and attraction.

1. Ailurophilia	:	love of cats
2. Ammophilous	:	sand-loving; preferring to dwell in sand
3. Anemophilous	:	pollinated by wind
4. Anglophilia	:	love or fondness for England or the English
5. Anthophilous	:	loving or frequenting flowers
6. Apodysophilia	:	feverish desire to undress
7. Astrophile	:	person interested in astronomy
8. Audiophile	:	one who loves accurately reproduced recorded sound
9. Belonephilia	:	sexual obsession with sharp objects
10. Bibliophily	:	love or fondness for books or reading
11. Canophilia	:	love or fondness for dogs
12. Cartophily	:	the hobby of collecting cigarette cards
13. Chasmophilous	:	fond of nooks, crevices and crannies
14. Chrysophilist	:	gold-lover
15. Clinophilia	:	passion for beds
16. Coprophilia	:	abnormal love or fondness for feces
17. Cynophilist	:	one who loves dogs
18. Dendrophilous	:	fond of trees
19. Discophile	:	one who loves and studies sound recordings
20. Electrophile	:	substance having an affinity for electrons or negative charge
21. Ergophile	:	one who loves work
22. Europhile	:	one who loves Europe

23.	Francophile	:	one who loves France or the French
24.	Gallophile	:	one who loves France or the French
25.	Germanophilia	:	love or fondness for Germany or the Germans
26.	Gerontophilia	:	sexual attraction towards the elderly
27.	Gynotikolobo-massophile	:	one who nibbles on women's earlobes
28.	Haemophilia	:	hereditary disease causing excesssive bleeding
29.	Halophilous	:	tolerant of salt or salt-water
30.	Heliophilous	:	preferring or attracted to the sunlight
31.	Hippophile	:	lover of horses
32.	Homophile	:	one who prefers the company of the same sex; a homosexual
33.	Hydrophilous	:	loving or preferring water
34.	Hygrophilous	:	preferring or living where there is an abundance of moisture
35.	Iconophilism	:	a taste for pictures and symbols
36.	Japanophilia	:	love or admiration for Japan or the Japanese
37.	Labeorphily	:	collection and study of beer bottle labels
38.	Lithophilous	:	living among stones
39.	Logophile	:	a lover of words
40.	Lygophilia	:	love of darkness
41.	Lyophile	:	easily dispersed in a suitable medium

42. Myrmecophilous	:	having a symbiotic relationship with ants
43. Necrophilia	:	unusual love or sexual attraction for corpses
44. Negrophile	:	one who is sympathetic towards black people
45. Neophile	:	one who loves novelty and trends
46. Nitrophilous	:	flourishing in or preferring locations with abundant nitrogen
47. Notaphily	:	collecting of bank-notes and cheques
48. Oenophile	:	one who is fond of or loves wine
49. Ombrophilous	:	tolerant of large amounts of rainfall
50. Ophiophilist	:	snake-lover
51. Paedophilia	:	abnormal love or sexual attraction for children
52. Palaeophile	:	antiquarian
53. Peristerophily	:	pigeon-collecting
54. Petrophilous	:	living on or thriving in rocky areas
55. Philalethist	:	lover of truth
56. Philately	:	study of postage stamps
57. Philhippic	:	loving or admiring horses
58. Phillumeny	:	collecting of matchbox labels
59. Philodemic	:	fond of commoners or the lower classes
60. Philogyny	:	love of women
61. Philomath	:	lover of learning
62. Philonoist	:	one who seeks knowledge
63. Philopornist	:	lover of prostitutes
64. Philotechnical	:	devoted to the arts

65. Philotherianism : love of animals
66. Philoxenia : hospitality
67. Photophilous : preferring or thriving in lighted conditions
68. Phytophilous : fond of plants
69. Pogonophile : one who loves beards
70. Psammophile : sand-loving plant
71. Psychrophilic : thriving in cold temperatures
72. Retrophilia : love of things of the past
73. Rheophile : living or thriving in running water
74. Rhizophilous : growing or thriving on or near roots
75. Russophile : one who admires Russia or the Russians
76. Sarcophilous : fond of flesh
77. Sciophilous : thriving in or loving shady conditions
78. Scopophilia : obtaining sexual pleasure from seeing things
79. Scotophilia : admiration for Scotland or the Scots
80. Scripophily : collection of bond and share certificates
81. Sinophil : one who admires China or the Chinese
82. Slavophile : one who admires the Slavs
83. Spermophile : member of family of seed-loving rodents
84. Stegophilist : one who climbs buildings for sport
85. Stigmatophilia : obsession with tattooing or branding

86. Symphily : living together for mutual benefit
87. Technophile : one who is fond of technology
88. Thalassophilous : living in or fond of the sea
89. Theophile : one who loves or is loved by God
90. Thermophilous : preferring or thriving in high temperatures
91. Timbrophily : love or fondness for stamps; stamp collecting
92. Tobaccophile : one who loves tobacco
93. Topophilia : great love or affection for a particular place
94. Toxophily : love of archery; study of archery.
95. Turophile : cheese lover
96. Typhlophile : one who is kind to the blind
97. Xenophilia : love of foreigners
98. Xerophily : adaptation to very dry conditions
99. Xylophilous : fond of wood; living in or on wood
100. Zoophilia : loving or caring for animals; bestiality

One-Word Substitutes For Various Types Of Fighting

In Greek the word *mache* means to fight. In English there are certain words that have the suffix – *machy* derived from the Greek word *mache*. These words, which are not very common are used to mean fighting, combat and conflict. A list of one words for various fights are given below.

1. Alectryomachy : cock-fighting
2. Duomachy : duel or fight between two people
3. Gigantomachy : war of giants against the gods
4. Hieromachy : fight or quarrel between priests
5. Logomachy : contention about words or in words

6. Monomachy : single combat; a duel
7. Naumachy : mock sea-battle
8. Poetomachia : contest or quarrel among poets
9. Pygmachy : boxing; fighting with clubs
10. Pyromachy : use of fire in combat
11. Skiamachy : sham fight; shadow boxing
12. Symmachy : fighting jointly against a common enemy
13. Tauromachy : bullfighting
14. Theomachy : war amongst or against the gods
15. Titanomachy : war of the Titans against the gods

One-Word Substitute For Used In Ecclesiastics

There are a wide range of obscure one-word related to Christian churches, priests, prayers, objects. Here is a list of these uncommon words.

1. Abthane : monastic region of the old Irish church
2. Adiaphoron : tenet or belief on which the logical system is indifferent
3. Adoptionism : belief that Christ was the adopted and not natural son of God
4. Advowson : right of presentation to church living
5. Adytum : sacred part of a temple or church; church chancel
6. Affusion : pouring on; as of baptismal water
7. Agapeselfless : Christian love; a feast in celebration of such love
8. Almoner : giver of alms; social worker in a hospital
9. Altarage : Day of Goodwill (December 26)

Kwanzaa (December 26 to January 1) payment to priest for mass;
offerings at altar

10. Ambo : early Christian raised reading desk or pulpit
11. Ambry : recess for church vessels; cupboard or niche
12. Ambulatory : aisle down the east end of a church
13. Amice : strip of fine linen worn as cloak or wrap by priest at mass
14. Ampulla : vessel for holy oil or wine for coronations or rituals
15. Anamnesis : reminiscence; prayer recalling death and resurrection of Jesus
16. Anchorite : one withdrawn from the world for religious reasons
17. Antependium : covering or cloth over pulpit or altar
18. Antilegomena : books of the New Testament not part of early Christian Bible
19. Antipedobaptism : denial of validity of infant baptism
20. Antiphon : anthem sung as a response during Church service
21. Apocatastasis : final restitution of all things at the appearance of the Messiah
22. Auto-da-fe : burning of a heretic
23. Autotheism : belief that one is God incarnate or that one is Christ
24. Baldaquin : covering or canopy over a throne or altar

25.	Baptistery	:	part of Church reserved for performing baptisms
26.	Beadle	:	Church caretaker or usher
27.	Beadsman	:	monk or almoner who prays for benefactor
28.	Bema	:	raised part of an Eastern Church containing the altar
29.	Benefice	:	ecclesiastical office to which revenue is attached
30.	Bethel	:	a place of worship for seamen; non-conformist chapel
31.	Biretta	:	square three-ridged cap worn by Catholic clergy
32.	Reviary	:	book containing daily Church service
33.	Bulla	:	round seal attached to a papal bull
34.	Bullantic	:	capitalized and ornamented, as letters used on papal bulls
35.	Bullary	:	collection of papal bulls
36.	Bursary	:	treasury of a monastery or college
37.	Burse	:	square cloth case to carry the corporal during Communion service
38.	Campanile	:	freestanding bell tower on Church property
39.	Canoness	:	woman living in a community under a religious rule
40.	Canticle	:	short holy song or sung prayer
41.	Catabaptism	:	belief in the wrongness of infant baptism

42.	Catechumen	:	one undergoing instruction prior to conversion to Christianity
43.	Cathedra	:	chair or throne of office for a bishop or other high official
44.	Cenacle	:	room where the Last Supper was eaten
45.	Cenobite	:	monk; member of religious group
46.	Cenoby	:	monastery or convent
47.	Censer	:	vessel for burning incense in religious rituals
48.	Cephalophore	:	decapitated saint depicted with head tucked under arm
49.	Chancel	:	part of church containing altar and seats for choir
50.	Chancery	:	Church office dealing with legal matters and archives
51.	Chantry	:	chapel or altar built for prayers for its benefactor's soul
52.	Chaplet	:	circlet or wreath for the head; short string of prayer beads
53.	Chasuble	:	sleeveless ecclesiastical garment
54.	Chevet	:	east end of a Church
55.	Chiliasm	:	belief that Jesus will reign on Earth for a thousand years
56.	Chimere	:	loose sleeveless robes worn by Anglican bishops
57.	Chrism	:	consecrated or holy oil
58.	Chrismation	:	sacrament of baptism in Eastern Churches
59.	Chrismatory	:	vessel for holding holy oil
60.	Cincture	:	to gird or surround; belt worn around ecclesiastical vestment

61. Cingulum : girdle or girdle-like structure; priest's belt
62. Circumincession : the reciprocal existence of three parts of the Trinity in each other
63. Clerestory : upper storey of a Church; windows near the roof of a building
64. Coadjutor : bishop assisting a diocesan bishop and having the right of succession
65. Collegialism : theory that Church is independent from the state
66. Colporteur : peddler of religious tracts and books
67. Compaternity : spiritual relationship between child's parents and godparents
68. Compline : prayer service held just before bedtime
69. Comprecation : prayer meeting
70. Concelebrate : to jointly recite the canon of the Eucharist in unison with others
71. Concordat : agreement between the pope and a secular government
72. Confirmand : candidate for religious confirmation
73. Confiteor : prayer of confession of sins
74. Consistory : a solemn assembly or council; a Church tribunal
75. Consultor : advisor to a Catholic bishop

76. Conventicle : secret or illegal Church assembly
77. Corporal : white cloth on which Communion bread and wine are placed
78. Credence : small table for holding sacred vessels
79. Credo : concise statement of doctrine; section of Mass followed by offertory
80. Curate : assistant to a parish priest
81. Curia : papal court and its officials
82. Dalmatic : ecclesiastical robe or other outer vestment
83. Datary : papal officer who registers and dates bulls and edicts
84. Decanal : located on south side of the choir in a Church
85. Decretal : papal decree deciding a point of Church law
86. Deiparous : bearing a god
87. Deodate : gift to or from God
88. Diaconicon : sacristy for sacred vessels in Orthodox churches
89. Diphysitism : belief in the dual nature of Christ
90. Doxology : hymn or verse of praise to God
91. Dulia : inferior veneration of saints and angels in comparison with God
92. Ecclesiastry : affairs of the Church
93. Eirenics : theological doctrine of religious unification
94. Encolpion : reliquary; cross worn on the breast

95.	Encyclical	:	letter sent by the pope to multiple bishops
96.	Eparchy	:	diocese of an Eastern Church
97.	Epiclesis	:	calling on the Holy Spirit to consecrate the Eucharist
98.	Exeat	:	permission from bishop for clergyman to work elsewhere
99.	Exequy	:	funeral rites; funeral procession
100.	Faldstool	:	desk from which the Litany is read at Church service
101.	Fanion	:	cloth worn on priest's arm and used for handling holy vessels
102.	Fenestella	:	recess in Church wall for storing communion vessels
103.	Feretory	:	shrine for relics during a procession or for a funeral bier
104.	Feria	:	weekday of a Church calendar on which no holiday falls
105.	Hagioscope	:	opening in wall to enable viewing of altar
106.	Hanap	:	chalice used in communion whose cover is a second chalice
107.	Hassock	:	kneeling cushion in a Church
108.	Hearsecloth	:	cloth lain over coffin during funeral
109.	Hgumene	:	head of a nunnery
110.	Hieratical	:	priestly; bound by religious convention
111.	Hieromonach	:	monk who also serves as a priest
112.	Holobaptism	:	belief in baptism with total immersion in water

113. Homolegomena : books of the Bible used in early Christianity
114. Housel : the eucharist; the act of taking the eucharist
115. Hymnal : collection of Church hymns
116. Hymnody : hymns collectively; hymn-singing
117. Hyperdulia : veneration of the Virgin Mary above saints and angels
118. Iconostasis : screen or partition in Eastern Churches with tiers of icons
119. Internuncio : messenger between two parties; low-ranking papal legate
120. Intinction : administering communion by dipping bread into wine
121. Introit : psalm or hymn sung at beginning of Church service
122. Invination : presence of Christ's blood in sanctified wine
123. Irrelevant : having no connection with the subject at issue.
124. Jubilarian : one who celebrates a jubilee, especially a priest, monk, or nun
125. Jubilate : the third Sunday after Easter
126. Kamelaukion : tall cylindrical hat worn by Orthodox priests
127. Kerygma : preaching of the Christian gospel
128. Kerygmatic : of, like or pertaining to preaching the Gospel
129. Kirking : first attendance of a couple at Church after marriage
130. Kyrie : religious petition for mercy

131.	Lavabo	:	ceremony in which priest washes his hands; basin for the ceremony
132.	Lavatory	:	wash-basin for washing bodies of newly dead; room where lavabo is kept
133.	Lavra	:	group of recluses' cells
134.	Lectern	:	desk or stand from which Church lessons are read
135.	Lection	:	reading; lesson read in Church
136.	Lectrice	:	female reader in Church
137.	Litany	:	prayer of supplication in responsive style
138.	Liturgician	:	one who studies or recites Church rituals
139.	Locum	:	clergyman temporarily replacing regular priest
140.	Lustration	:	ritual washing; ablution
141.	Lychgate	:	roofed gate of a Churchyard
142.	Mancipl e	:	steward of a college or monastery; purveyor
143.	Mariolatry	:	worship of the virgin mother
144.	Mariology	:	study of the Virgin Mary
145.	Marrano	:	Jew converted to Christianity to avoid persecution
146.	Martyrology	:	study of martyrs
147.	Mendicant	:	member of impoverished religious order
148.	Messianism	:	belief in a single messiah or saviour
149.	Modalism	:	belief in unity of Father, Son and Holy Spirit

150.	Monophysitism	:	belief that Christ was primarily divine but in human form
151.	Monotheletism	:	belief that Christ had only one will
152.	Monstrance	:	vessel used to expose the Eucharist
153.	Nipter	:	ecclesiastical ceremony of washing the feet
154.	Nones	:	prayer service held at 3 p.m.
155.	Novena	:	series of Catholic Church services held on nine successive days
156.	Orarium	:	book of private devotions
157.	Osculatory	:	carved tablet kissed by priest during celebration of mass
158.	Ostensory	:	container for holding consecrated communion wafers
159.	Paedobaptism	:	doctrine of infant baptism
160.	Pallium	:	white woollen band symbolising archbishop's authority
161.	Panegyricon	:	collection of sermons for Orthodox Church festivals
162.	Pannychis	:	an attendent of God
163.	Recusant	:	one who refuses to attend catholic Church services; nonconformist
164.	Refectory	:	dining-hall of a monastery or other institution
165.	Regula	:	rule of a religious order
166.	Requiescat	:	prayer for the dead
167.	Rescript	:	answer of pope or emperor to any legal question; edict or decree

168. Responsory : set of responses sung or said after liturgical reading
169. Retable : self or ornamental setting for panels behind an altar
170. Retrochoir : space in choir behind high altar
171. Sacristy : room in Church where sacred objects are kept
172. Schola : Church choir led by a cantor
173. Scholasticate : preparatory college for those intending to enter Catholic order
174. Sempect : extremely elderly Benedictine monk
175. Sepulchre : receptacle in an altar for holding religious relics
176. Sext : prayer service held at noon
177. Slype : covered passage between walls, or between transept and chapterhouse
178. Soteriology : study of theological salvation
179. Suffragan : assistant bishop
180. Taperer : one who bears a taper during a religious procession
181. Terce : prayer service held at 9 a.m.
182. Theanthroposophy : system of belief concerning Christ as god and man
183. Theodidact : student of God; one who is taught by God
184. Theody : hymn in praise of God
185. Theolepsy : seizure or possession by a God
186. Theometry : measurement or estimation of God

187.	Theophany	:	manifestation or appearance of a God to people
188.	Transub-stantiation	:	miraculous changing of bread and wine into body and blood of Christ
189.	Trental	:	commemoratory service held thirty days after burial
190.	Tympanum	:	space within an arch; arched recess at entrance of cathedral
191.	Ubiquitarianism	:	belief that Christ is everywhere
192.	Unalist	:	priest holding one benefice
193.	Vernicle	:	cloth with image of Christ's face impressed upon it
194.	Versicle	:	short verse in Church service normally followed by response
195.	Vespers	:	prayer service held in early evening
196.	Vesturer	:	keeper of vestments
197.	Wicket	:	small door forming part of larger door of a Church or castle
198.	Wimple	:	cloth covering for head and neck worn by nuns
199.	Xerophagy	:	eating of dry food; fast of dry food in the week preceding Easter
200.	zeta	:	small room or closet in a Church

□

One-Word Substitutes Related To Unusual Arts

Man has an ardent desire of practicing various superstitions, divinations and art forms, including fortune telling, runes, tarot cards reading, horoscopes, gemology, numerology, etc. People have developed various practices to use to predict the future. Therefore a wide range of words have been formulated to describe their practices. Some of the words end in *-mancy,* which is adopted from the Greek word *manteia*, meaning divination.

1. Acultomancy : divination using needless.
2. Aeromancy : divination by means of the weather
3. Ailuromancy : divination by watching cats' movements
4. Alectormancy : divination by sacrificing a rooster
5. Alectryomancy : divination by watching a rooster gather corn kernels
6. Aleuromancy : divination using flour or meal
7. Aalomancy : divination using salt
8. Alphitomancy : divination using loaves of barley
9. Alveromancy : divination using sounds
10. Ambulomancy : divination by taking a walk

11. Amniomancy	:	divination by examining afterbirth
12. Anthomancy	:	divination using flowers
13. Anthracomancy	:	divination using burning coals
14. Anthropomancy	:	divination using human entrails
15. Apantomancy	:	divination using objects at hand
16. Arithmancy	:	divination using numbers
17. Armomancy	:	divination by examining one's shoulders
18. Aspidomancy	:	divination by sitting and chanting within a circle
19. Astragalomancy	:	divination using dice or knucklebones
20. Astromancy	:	divination using stars
21. Austromancy	:	divination using wind
22. Axinomancy	:	divination using an axe or hatchet
23. Batraquomancy	:	divination using frogs
24. Belomancy	:	divination by means of arrows
25. Bibliomancy	:	divination by opening a book at random
26. Botanomancy	:	divination using burning branches or plants
27. Brontomancy	:	divination using thunder
28. Capnomancy	:	divination by means of smoke
29. Cartomancy	:	telling fortunes using playing cards
30. Catoptromancy	:	divination by examining mirror placed underwater
31. Causimancy	:	divination by means of fire
32. Ceneromancy	:	divination using ashes
33. Cephalonomancy	:	divination by boiling an ass head
34. Ceraunomancy	:	divination using thunderbolts

35. Ceraunoscopy : divination using lightning
36. Ceromancy : divination by means of wax drippings
37. Ceroscopy : divination using wax
38. Chaomancy : divination by examining phenomena of the air
39. Chirognomy : divination by studying the hands
40. Chiromancy : divination by means of palmistry
41. Chronomancy : divination by means of time
42. Cleidomancy : divination using keys
43. Cleromancy : divination using dice
44. Conchomancy : divination using shells
45. Coscinomancy : divination using a sieve and a pair of shears
46. Crithomancy : divination by strewing meal over sacrifices
47. Critomancy : divination using viands and cakes
48. Cromnyomancy : divination using onions
49. Crystallomancy : divination by means of clear objects
50. Crystalomancy : divination using a crystal globe
51. Cubomancy : divination by throwing dice
52. Dactyliomancy : divination by means of a finger
53. Daphnomancy : divination using a laurel
54. Demonomancy : divination using demons
55. Dririmancy : divination by observing dripping blood
56. Emonomancy : divination using demons
57. Enoptromancy : divination using mirrors
58. Eromancy : divination using water vessels
59. Extispicy : divination using entrails
60. Floromancy : belief that flowers have feelings

61. Gastromancy : divination by sounds from the belly
62. Geloscopy : fortune-telling by means of laughter
63. Geomancy : divination by casting earth onto a surface
64. Grafology : divination by studying writing
65. Graptomancy : divination by studying handwriting
66. Gyromancy : divination by falling from dizziness
67. Halomancy : divination using salt
68. Haruspication : divination by inspecting animal entrails
69. Hematomancy : divination using blood
70. Hepatoscopy : divination by examining animal livers
71. Hieromancy : divination by studying objects offered in sacrifice
72. Hieroscopy : divination using entrails
73. Hippomancy : divination using horses
74. Hydromancy : divination using water
75. Hypnomancy : divination using sleep
76. Ichnomancy : divination using footprints
77. Ichthyomancy : divination by inspecting fish entrails
78. Iconomancy : divination using icons
79. Idolomancy : divination using idols
80. Kephalonomancy : divination using a baked ass's head
81. Keraunoscopia : divination using thunder
82. Knissomancy : divination using burning incense

83. Labiomancy : lip reading
84. Lampadomancy : divination by flame
85. Lecanomancy : divination using water in a basin or pool
86. Libanomancy : divination by watching incense smoke
87. Lithomancy : divination by stones or meteorites
88. Logarithmancy : divination by means of algorithms
89. Logomancy : divination using words
90. Macromancy : divination using large objects
91. Maculomancy : divination using spots
92. Margaritomancy : divination using pearls
93. Mathemancy : divination by counting
94. Meconomancy : divination using sleep
95. Meteoromancy : divination by studying meteors
96. Metopomancy : divination using the forehead or face
97. Metoposcopy : fortune-telling or judgement of character by the lines of the forehead
98. Micromancy : divination using small objects
99. Myomancy : divination from the movements of mice
100. Narcomancy : divination using sleep
101. Necyomancy : divination by summoning Satan
102. Nomancy : divination by examining letters of name
103. Odontomancy : divination using teeth
104. Oenomancy : divination by studying appearance of wine
105. Oinomancy : divination using wine

106.	Ololygmancy	:	fortune-telling by the howling of dogs
107.	Omoplatoscopy	:	divination by observing cracks in burning scapulae
108.	Omphalomancy	:	divination from the knots in the umbilical cord
109.	Oneiromancy	:	divination by dreams
110.	Onomancy	:	divination using proper names
111.	Onychomancy	:	divination by the fingernails
112.	Onymancy	:	divination by the fingernails
113.	Oomancy	:	divination using eggs
114.	Ophidiomancy	:	divination using snakes
115.	Ophiomancy	:	divination by watching snakes
116.	Ornithomancy	:	divination by observing flight of birds
117.	Oryctomancy	:	divination using excavated objects
118.	Ossomancy	:	divination using bones
119.	Ouranomancy	:	divination using the heavens
120.	Pedomancy	:	divination by examining the soles of the feet
121.	Pegomancy	:	divination by springs or fountains
122.	Pessomancy	:	divination using pebbles
123.	Phyllomancy	:	divination using leaves or tea leaves
124.	Physiognomancy	:	divination by studying the face
125.	Psephomancy	:	divination by drawing lots or markers at random
126.	Psychomancy	:	divination by means of spirits
127.	Pyromancy	:	divination using fire
128.	Retromancy	:	divination by looking over one's shoulder

129. Rhabdomancy : divination using a rod or stick
130. Rhapsodomancy : divination by opening works of poetry at random
131. Scapulomancy : divination by examining burnt shoulder blade
132. Scatomancy : divination by studying excrement
133. Scatoscopy : divination by studying excrement; scatomancy
134. Schematomancy : divination using the human form
135. Sciomancy : divination using ghosts
136. Scyphomancy : divination by means of a cup
137. Selenomancy : divination by studying the moon
138. Sideromancy : divination using stars; divination by burning straws
139. Sortilege : divination by drawing lots
140. Spasmatomancy : divination by twitching or convulsions of the body
141. Spatilomancy : divination by means of feces
142. Spheromancy : divination using a crystal ball
143. Spodomancy : divination by means of ashes
144. Stercomancy : fortune-telling by studying seeds in dung
145. Stichomancy : divination by picking passages from books at random
146. Stolisomancy : divination by observing how one dresses oneself
147. Sycomancy : divination using fig leaves
148. Tephromancy : divination by ashes
149. Theomancy : divination by means of oracles
150. Thrioboly : divination using pebbles
151. Thumomancy : divination by means of one's own soul

152. Tiromancy : divination using cheese
153. Topomancy : divination using landforms
154. Trochomancy : divination by studying wheel tracks
155. Tyromancy : divination using cheese
156. Uranomancy : divination by studying the heavens
157. Urimancy : divination by observing urine
158. Xenomancy : divination using strangers
159. Xylomancy : divination by examining wood found in one's path
160. Zoomancy : divination by observing animals

□

7

One-Word Substitutes For Studies And Sciences

People are interested in studying a wide range of subjects. Various subject names are used to talk about different branches of scientific studies. Some uncommon one-words substitutes representing scientific studies are listed below.

1. Arctophily : study of teddybears
2. Areology : study of mars
3. Arthrology : study of joints
4. Astheniology : study of diseases of weakening and aging
5. Astrogeology : study of extraterrestrial geology
6. Astrology : study of influence of stars on people
7. Astrometeorology : study of effect of stars on climate
8. Astronomy : study of celestial bodies
9. Astrophysics : study of behaviour of interstellar matter
10. Astroseismology : study of star oscillations
11. Atmology : the science of aqueous vapour
12. Audiology : study of hearing
13. Autecology : study of ecology of one species

14. Autology : scientific study of oneself
15. Auxology : science of growth
16. Avionics : the science of electronic devices for aircraft
17. Axiology : the science of the ultimate nature of values
18. Bacteriology : study of bacteria
19. Balneology : the science of the therapeutic use of baths
20. Barodynamics : science of the support and mechanics of bridges
21. Barology : study of gravitation
22. Batology : the study of brambles
23. Bibliology : study of books
24. Bibliotics : study of documents to determine authenticity
25. Bioecology : study of interaction of life in the environment
26. Biology : study of life
27. Biometrics : study of biological measurement
28. Bionomics : study of organisms interacting in their environments
29. Botany : study of plants
30. Bromatology : study of food
31. Brontology : scientific study of thunder
32. Bryology : the study of mosses and liverworts
33. Cacogenics : study of racial degeneration

34. Caliology : study of bird's nests
35. Calorifics : study of heat
36. Cambistry : science of international exchange
37. Campanology : the art of bell ringing
38. Carcinology : study of crabs and other crustaceans
39. Cardiology : study of the heart
40. Caricology : study of sedges
41. Carpology : study of fruit
42. Cartography : the science of making maps and globes
43. Castrametation : the art of designing a camp
44. Catacoustics : science of echoes or reflected sounds
45. Catalactics : science of commercial exchange
46. Catechectics : the art of teaching by question and answer
47. Cetology : study of whales and dolphins
48. Chalcography : the art of engraving on copper or brass
49. Chalcotriptics : art of taking rubbings from ornamental brasses
50. Chaology : the study of chaos or chaos theory
51. Characterology : study of development of character
52. Chemistry : study of properties of substances
53. Chirocosmetics : beautifying the hands; art of manicure
54. Chirography : study of handwriting or penmanship

55. Chirology : study of the hands
56. Chiropody : medical science of feet
57. Chorology : science of the geographic description of anything
58. Chrematistics : the study of wealth; political economy
59. Chronobiology : study of biological rhythms
60. Chrysology : study of precious metals
61. Ciselure : the art of chasing metal
62. Climatology : study of climate
63. Clinology : study of aging or individual decline after maturity
64. Codicology : study of manuscripts
65. Coleopterology : study of beetles and weevils
66. Cometology : study of comets
67. Conchology : study of shells
68. Coprology : study of pornography
69. Cosmetology : study of cosmetics
70. Cosmology : study of the universe
71. Craniology : study of the skull
72. Criminology : study of crime; criminals
73. Cryobiology : study of life under cold conditions
74. Cryptology : study of codes
75. Cryptozoology : study of animals for whose existence there is no conclusive proof
76. Ctetology : study of the inheritance of acquired characteristics
77. Cynology : scientific study of dogs
78. Cytology : study of living cells
79. Dactyliology : study of rings

80. Dactylography : the study of fingerprints
81. Dactylology : study of sign language
82. Deltiology : the collection and study of picture postcards
83. Demology : study of human behaviour
84. Demonology : study of demons
85. Dendrochronology : study of tree rings
86. Deontology : the theory or study of moral obligation
87. Dermatoglyphics : the study of skin patterns and fingerprints
88. Dermatology : study of skin
89. Desmology : study of ligaments
90. Diabology : study of devils
91. Diagraphics : art of making diagrams or drawings
92. Dialectology : study of dialects
93. Dioptrics : study of light refraction
94. Diplomatics : science of deciphering ancient writings and texts
95. Diplomatology : study of diplomats
96. Docimology : the art of assaying
97. Dosiology : the study of doses
98. Dramaturgy : art of producing and staging dramatic works
99. Dysgenics : the study of racial degeneration
100. Dysteleology : study of purposeless organs
101. Ecclesiology : study of Church affairs
102. Eccrinology : study of excretion
103. Ecology : study of environment
104. Economics : study of material wealth
105. Edaphology : study of soils

106. Egyptology : study of ancient egypt
107. Ekistics : study of human settlement
108. Electrochemistry : study of relations between electricity and chemicals
109. Electrology : study of electricity
110. Electrostatics : study of static electricity
111. Embryology : study of embryos
112. Emetology : study of vomiting
113. Emmenology : the study of menstruation
114. Endemiology : study of local diseases
115. Endocrinology : study of glands
116. Enigmatology : study of enigmas
117. Entomology : study of insects
118. Entozoology : study of parasites that live inside larger organisms
119. Enzymology : study of enzymes
120. Ephebiatrics : branch of medicine dealing with adolescence
121. Epidemiology : study of diseases; epidemics
122. Epileptology : study of epilepsy
123. Epistemology : study of grounds of knowledge
124. Eremology : study of deserts
125. Ergology : study of effects of work on humans
126. Ergonomics : study of people at work
127. Escapology : study of freeing oneself from constraints
128. Eschatology : study of death; final matters
129. Ethnogeny : study of origins of races or ethnic groups
130. Ethnology : study of cultures

131. Ethnomethodology : study of everyday communication
132. Ethnomusicology : study of comparative musical systems
133. Ethology : study of natural or biological character
134. Ethonomics : study of economic and ethical principles of a society
135. Etiology : the science of causes; especially of disease
136. Etymology : study of origins of words
137. Euthenics : science concerned with improving living conditions
138. Exobiology : study of extraterrestrial life
139. Floristry : the art of cultivating and selling flowers
140. Fluviology : study of watercourses
141. Folkloristics : study of folklore and fables
142. Futurology : study of future
143. Garbology : study of garbage
144. Gastroenterology : study of stomach; intestines
145. Gastronomy : study of fine dining
146. Gemmology : study of gems and jewels
147. Genealogy : study of descent of families
148. Genesiology : study of reproduction and heredity
149. Genethlialogy : the art of casting horoscopes
150. Geochemistry : study of chemistry of the earth's crust
151. Geochronology : study of measuring geological time

152. Geogeny : science of the formation of the earth's crust
153. Geography : study of surface of the earth and its inhabitants
154. Geology : study of earth's crust
155. Geomorphogeny : study of the origins of land forms
156. Geoponics : study of agriculture
157. Geotechnics : study of increasing habitability of the earth
158. Geratology : study of decadence and decay
159. Gerocomy : study of old age
160. Gerontology : study of the elderly; aging
161. Gigantology : study of giants
162. Glaciology : study of ice ages and glaciation
163. Glossology : study of language; study of the tongue
164. Glyptography : the art of engraving on gems
165. Glyptology : study of gem engravings
166. Gnomonics : the art of measuring time using sundials
167. Gnosiology : study of knowledge; philosophy of knowledge
168. Gnotobiology : study of life in germ-free conditions
169. Graminology : study of grasses
170. Grammatology : study of systems of writing
171. Graphemics : study of systems of representing speech in writing
172. Graphology : study of handwriting
173. Gromatics : science of surveying
174. Gynaecology : study of women's physiology

175. Gyrostatics : the study of rotating bodies
176. Haemataulics : study of movement of blood through blood vessels
177. Hagiology : study of saints
178. Halieutics : study of fishing
179. Hamartiology : study of sin
180. Harmonics : study of musical acoustics
181. Hedonics : part of ethics or psychology dealing with pleasure
182. Helcology : study of ulcers
183. Heliology : science of the sun
184. Helioseismology : study of sun's interior by observing its surface oscillations
185. Helminthology : study of worms
186. Hematology : study of blood
187. Heortology : study of religious feasts
188. Hepatology : study of liver
189. Heraldry : study of coats of arms
190. Heresiology : study of heresies
191. Herpetology : study of reptiles and amphibians
192. Hierology : science of sacred matters
193. Hippiatrics : study of diseases of horses
194. Hippology : the study of horses
195. Histology : study of the tissues of organisms
196. Histopathology : study of changes in tissue due to disease
197. Historiography : study of writing history
198. Historiology : study of history
199. Hoplology : the study of weapons
200. Horography : art of constructing sundials or clocks
201. Horology : science of time measurement

202. Horticulture : study of gardening
203. Hydrobiology : study of aquatic organisms
204. Hydrodynamics : study of movement in liquids
205. Hydrogeology : study of ground water
206. Hydrography : study of investigating bodies of water
207. Hydrokinetics : study of motion of fluids
208. Hydrology : study of water resources
209. Hydrometeorology : study of atmospheric moisture
210. Hydropathy : study of treating diseases with water
211. Hyetology : science of rainfall
212. Hygiastics : science of health and hygiene
213. Hygienics : study of sanitation; health
214. Hygiology : hygienics; study of cleanliness
215. Hygrology : study of humidity
216. Hygrometry : science of humidity
217. Hymnography : study of writing hymns
218. Hymnology : study of hymns
219. Hypnology : study of sleep; study of hypnosis
220. Hypsography : science of measuring heights
221. Iamatology : study of remedies
222. Iatrology : treatise or text on medical topics; study of medicine
223. Iatromathematics : archaic practice of medicine in conjunction with astrology
224. Ichnography : art of drawing ground plans; a ground plan
225. Ichnology : science of fossilized footprints
226. Ichthyology : study of fish
227. Iconography : study of drawing symbols
228. Iconology : study of icons; symbols

229. Ideogeny : study of origins of ideas
230. Ideology : science of ideas; system of ideas used to justify behaviour
231. Idiomology : study of idiom, jargon or dialect
232. Idiopsychology : psychology of one's own mind
233. Immunogenetics : study of genetic characteristics of immunity
234. Immunology : study of immunity
235. Immunopathology : study of immunity to disease
236. Insectology : study of insects
237. Irenology : the study of peace
238. Iridology : study of the iris; diagnosis of disease based on the iris of the eye
239. Kalology : study of beauty
240. Karyology : study of cell nuclei
241. Kidology : study of kidding
242. Kinematics : study of motion
243. Kinesics : study of gestural communication
244. Kinesiology : study of human movement and posture
245. Kinetics : study of forces producing or changing motion
246. Koniology : study of atmospheric pollutants and dust
247. Ktenology : science of putting people to death
248. Kymatology : study of wave motion
249. Labeorphily : collection and study of beer bottle labels
250. Larithmics : study of population statistics

251.	Laryngology	:	study of larynx
252.	Lepidopterology	:	study of butterflies and moths
253.	Leprology	:	study of leprosy
254.	Lexicology	:	study of words and their meanings
255.	Lexigraphy	:	art of definition of words
256.	Lichenology	:	study of lichens
257.	Limacology	:	study of slugs
258.	Limnobiology	:	study of freshwater ecosystems
259.	Limnology	:	study of bodies of fresh water
260.	Linguistics	:	study of language
261.	Lithology	:	study of rocks
262.	Liturgiology	:	study of liturgical forms and Church rituals
263.	Loimology	:	study of plagues and epidemics
264.	Loxodromy	:	study of sailing along rhumb-lines
265.	Magirics	:	art of cookery
266.	Magnanerie	:	art of raising silkworms
267.	Magnetics	:	study of magnetism
268.	Malacology	:	study of molluscs
269.	Malariology	:	study of malaria
270.	Mammalogy	:	study of mammals
271.	Mariology	:	study of the Virgin Mary
272.	Martyrology	:	study of martyrs
273.	Mathematics	:	study of magnitude, number and forms
274.	Mazology	:	mammalogy; study of mammals
275.	Mechanics	:	study of action of force on bodies
276.	Meconology	:	study of or treatise concerning opium

277. Melittology : study of bees
278. Mereology : study of part-whole relationships
279. Mesology : ecology
280. Metallogeny : study of the origin and distribution of metal deposits
281. Metallography : study of the structure and constitution of metals
282. Metallurgy : study of alloying and treating metals
283. Metaphysics : study of principles of nature and thought
284. Metapolitics : study of politics in theory or abstract
285. Metapsychology : study of nature of the mind
286. Meteoritics : the study of meteors
287. Meteorology : study of weather
288. Metrics : study of versification
289. Metrology : science of weights and measures
290. Microanatomy : study of microscopic tissues
291. Microbiology : study of microscopic organisms
292. Microclimatology : study of local climates
293. Micrology : study or discussion of trivialities
294. Micropalaeontology : study of microscopic fossils
295. Microphytology : study of very small plant life
296. Microscopy : study of minute objects
297. Mineralogy : study of minerals
298. Molinology : study of mills and milling
299. Momilogy : study of mummies
300. Morphology : study of forms and the development of structures
301. Muscology : the study of mosses

302.	Museology	:	the study of museums
303.	Musicology	:	study of music
304.	Mycology	:	study of funguses
305.	Myology	:	study of muscles
306.	Myrmecology	:	study of ants
307.	Mythology	:	study of myths; fables; tales
308.	Naology	:	study of Church or temple architecture
309.	Nasology	:	study of the nose
310.	Nematology	:	the study of nematodes
311.	Neonatology	:	study of newborn babies
312.	Neossology	:	study of nestling birds
313.	Nephology	:	study of clouds
314.	Nephrology	:	study of the kidneys
315.	Neurobiology	:	study of anatomy of the nervous system
316.	Neurology	:	study of nervous system
317.	Neuropsychology	:	study of relation between brain and behaviour
318.	Neurypnology	:	study of hypnotism
319.	Neutrosophy	:	study of the origin and nature of philosophical neutralities
320.	Nidology	:	study of nests
321.	Nomology	:	the science of the laws; especially of the mind
322.	Noology	:	science of the intellect
323.	Nosology	:	study of diseases
324.	Nostology	:	study of senility
325.	Notaphily	:	collecting of bank-notes and cheques
326.	Numerology	:	study of numbers
327.	Numismatics	:	study of coins

328. Nymphology : study of nymphs
329. Obstetrics : study of midwifery
330. Oceanography : study of oceans
331. Odology : science of the hypothetical mystical force of God
332. Odontology : study of teeth
333. Oenology : study of wines
334. Oikology : science of housekeeping
335. Olfactology : study of the sense of smell
336. Ombrology : study of rain
337. Oncology : study of tumours
338. Oneirology : study of dreams
339. Onomasiology : study of nomenclature
340. Onomastics : study of proper names
341. Ontology : science of pure being; the nature of things
342. Oology : study of eggs
343. Ophiology : study of snakes
344. Ophthalmology : study of eye diseases
345. Optics : study of light
346. Optology : study of sight
347. Optometry : science of examining the eyes
348. Orchidology : study of orchids
349. Ornithology : study of birds
350. Orology : study of mountains
351. Orthoepy : study of correct pronunciation
352. Orthography : study of spelling
353. Orthopterology : study of cockroaches
354. Oryctology : mineralogy or paleontology
355. Osmics : scientific study of smells
356. Osmology : study of smells and olfactory processes

357.	Osphresiology	: study of the sense of smell
358.	Osteology	: study of bones
359.	Otology	: study of the ear
360.	Otorhinolaryngology	: study of ear, nose and throat
361.	Paedology	: study of children
362.	Paedotrophy	: art of rearing children
363.	Paidonosology	: study of children's diseases; pediatrics
364.	Palaeoanthropology	: study of early humans
365.	Palaeobiology	: study of fossil plants and animals
366.	Palaeoclimatology	: study of ancient climates
367.	Palaeolimnology	: study of ancient fish
368.	Palaeontology	: study of fossils
369.	Palaeopedology	: study of early soils
370.	Paleobotany	: study of ancient plants
371.	Paleo-osteology	: study of ancient bones
372.	Palynology	: study of pollen
373.	Papyrology	: study of paper
374.	Parapsychology	: study of unexplained mental phenomena
375.	Parasitology	: study of parasites
376.	Paroemiology	: study of proverbs
377.	Parthenology	: study of virgins
378.	Pataphysics	: the science of imaginary solutions
379.	Pathology	: study of disease
380.	Patrology	: study of early Christianity
381.	Pedagogics	: study of teaching
382.	Pedology	: study of soils
383.	Pelology	: study of mud
384.	Penology	: study of crime and punishment

385.	Periodontics	:	study of gums
386.	Pestology	:	science of pests
387.	Petrology	:	study of rocks
388.	Pharmacognosy	:	study of drugs of animal and plant origin
389.	Pharmacology	:	study of drugs
390.	Pharology	:	study of lighthouses
391.	Pharyngology	:	study of the throat
392.	Phenology	:	study of organisms as affected by climate
393.	Phenomenology	:	study of phenomena
394.	Philately	:	study of postage stamps
395.	Philematology	:	the act or study of kissing
396.	Phillumeny	:	collecting of matchbox labels
397.	Philology	:	study of ancient texts; historical linguistics
398.	Philosophy	:	science of knowledge or wisdom
399.	Phoniatrics	:	study and correction of speech defects
400.	Phonology	:	study of speech sounds
401.	Photobiology	:	study of effects of light on organisms
402.	Phraseology	:	study of phrases
403.	Phrenology	:	study of bumps on the head
404.	Phycology	:	study of algae and seaweeds
405.	Physics	:	study of properties of matter and energy
406.	Physiology	:	study of processes of life
407.	Phytology	:	study of plants; botany
408.	Piscatology	:	study of fishes
409.	Pisteology	:	science or study of faith

410. Planetology : study of planets
411. Plutology : political economy; study of wealth
412. Pneumatics : study of mechanics of gases
413. Podiatry : study and treatment of disorders of the foot; chiropody
414. Podology : study of the feet
415. Polemology : study of war
416. Pomology : study of fruit-growing
417. Posology : science of quantity or dosage
418. Potamology : study of rivers
419. Praxeology : study of practical or efficient activity; science of efficient action
420. Primatology : study of primates
421. Proctology : study of rectum
422. Prosody : study of versification
423. Protistology : study of protists
424. Proxemics : study of man's need for personal space
425. Psephology : study of election results and voting trends
426. Pseudoptics : study of optical illusions
427. Psychobiology : study of biology of the mind
428. Psychogenetics : study of internal or mental states
429. Psychognosy : study of mentality, personality or character
430. Psychology : study of mind
431. Psychopathology : study of mental illness
432. Psychophysics : study of link between mental and physical processes
433. Pteridology : study of ferns

434. Pterylology : study of distribution of feathers on birds

435. Pyretology : study of fevers

436. Pyrgology : study of towers

437. Pyroballogy : study of artillery

438. Pyrography : study of woodburning

439. Quinology : study of quinine

440. Raciology : study of racial differences

441. Radiology : study of X-rays and their medical applications

442. Reflexology : study of reflexes

443. Rhabdology : knowledge or learning concerning divining rods

444. Rhabdology : art of calculating using numbering rods

445. Rheology : science of the deformation or flow of matter

446. Rheumatology : study of rheumatism

447. Rhinology : study of the nose

448. Rhochrematics : science of inventory management and the movement of products

449. Runology : study of runes

450. Sarcology : study of fleshy parts of the body

451. Satanology : study of the devil

452. Scatology : study of excrement or obscene literature

453. Scripophily : collection of bond and share certificates

454. Sedimentology : study of sediment

455. Seismology : study of earthquakes

456.	Selenodesy	:	study of the shape and features of the moon
457.	Selenology	:	study of the moon
458.	Semantics	:	study of meaning
459.	Semasiology	:	study of meaning; semantics
460.	Semiology	:	study of signs and signals
461.	Semiotics	:	study of signs and symbols
462.	Serology	:	study of serums
463.	Sexology	:	study of sexual behaviour
464.	Sigillography	:	study of seals
465.	Significs	:	science of meaning
466.	Silvics	:	study of tree's life
467.	Sindonology	:	study of the shroud of Turin
468.	Sinology	:	study of China
469.	Sociobiology	:	study of biological basis of human behaviour
470.	Sociology	:	study of society
471.	Somatology	:	science of the properties of matter
472.	Sophiology	:	science of ideas
473.	Soteriology	:	study of theological salvation
474.	Spectrology	:	study of ghosts
475.	Spectroscopy	:	study of spectra
476.	Speleology	:	study and exploration of caves
477.	Spermology	:	study of seeds
478.	Sphagnology	:	study of peat moss
479.	Sphragistics	:	study of seals and signets
480.	Sphygmology	:	study of the pulse
481.	Splanchnology	:	study of the entrails or viscera
482.	Spongology	:	study of sponges
483.	Stasiology	:	study of political parties

484. Statics : study of bodies and forces in equilibrium
485. Stemmatology : study of relationships between texts
486. Stoichiology : science of elements of animal tissues
487. Stomatology : study of the mouth
488. Storiology : study of folktales
489. Stratigraphy : study of geological layers or strata
490. Stylometry : studying literature by means of statistical analysis
491. Suicidology : study of suicide
492. Symbology : study of symbols
493. Symptomatology : study of symptoms of illness
494. Synecology : study of ecological communities
495. Synectics : study of processes of invention
496. Syntax : study of sentence structure
497. Syphilology : study of syphilis
498. Systematology : study of systems
499. Tectonics : science of structure of objects, buildings and landforms
500. Tegestology : study and collecting of beer mats
501. Teleology : study of final causes; analysis in terms of purpose
502. Telmatology : study of swamps
503. Teratology : study of monsters, freaks, abnormal growths or malformations
504. Teuthology : study of cephalopods

505. Textology : study of the production of texts
506. Thalassography : science of the sea
507. Thanatology : study of death and its customs
508. Thaumatology : study of miracles
509. Theology : study of religion; religious doctrine
510. Theriatrics : veterinary medicine
511. Theriogenology : study of animals' reproductive systems
512. Thermodynamics : study of relation of heat to motion
513. Thermokinematics : study of motion of heat
514. Thermology : study of heat
515. Therology : study of wild mammals
516. Thremmatology : science of breeding domestic animals and plants
517. Threpsology : science of nutrition
518. Tidology : study of tides
519. Timbrology : study of postage stamps
520. Topology : study of places and their natural features
521. Toponymics : study of place-names
522. Toreutics : study of artistic work in metal
523. Toxicology : study of poisons
524. Toxophily : love of archery; archery; study of archery
525. Traumatology : study of wounds and their effects
526. Tribology : study of friction and wear between surfaces
527. Trichology : study of hair and its disorders

528. Trophology : study of nutrition
529. Tsiganology : study of gypsies
530. Typhlology : study of blindness and the blind
531. Typology : study of types of things
532. Ufology : study of alien spacecraft
533. Uranology : study of the heavens; astronomy
534. Urbanology : study of cities
535. Urenology : study of rust molds
536. Urology : study of urine; urinary tract
537. Venereology : study of venereal disease
538. Vermeology : study of worms
539. Vexillology : study of flags
540. Victimology : study of victims
541. Vinology : scientific study of vines and winemaking
542. Virology : study of viruses
543. Vitrics : glassy materials;glassware; study of glassware
544. Volcanology : study of volcanoes
545. Xylography : art of engraving on wood
546. Xylology : study of wood
547. Zenography : study of the planet Jupiter
548. Zooarchaeology : study of animal remains of archaeological sites
549. Zoogeography : study of geographic distribution of animals
550. Zoogeology : study of fossil animal remains
551. Zoology : study of animals
552. Zoonomy : animal physiology
553. Zoonosology : study of animal diseases
554. Zoophysiology : study of physiology of animals

555.	Zoophytology	:	study of plant-like animals
556.	Zoosemiotics	:	study of animal communication
557.	Zootaxy	:	science of classifying animals
558.	Zootechnics	:	science of breeding animals
559.	Zygology	:	science of joining and fastening
560.	Zymology	:	science of fermentation

□

8

One-Word Substitutes For Various Types Of Fear

Human beings often suffer from irrational or pathological fears of various things. There are several words that describe fear of certain things. Here is a list of Phobias.

1. Ablutophobia : fear of washing or bathing
2. Acarophobia : fear of itching or of the insects that cause itching and soon
3. Acerophobia : fear of sourness
4. Achluophobia : fear of darkness
5. Acousticophobia : fear of noise
6. Aerophobia : fear of drafts, air swallowing, or airbourne noxious substances
7. Aeroacrophobia : fear of open high places
8. Aeronausiphobia : fear of vomiting secondary to airsickness
9. Agateophobia : fear of insanity
10. Agliophobia : fear of pain
11. Agoraphobia : fear of open spaces or of being in crowded, public places like markets. Fear of leaving a safe place

12. Agraphobia : fear of sexual abuse
13. Agrizoophobia : fear of wild animals
14. Agyrophobia : fear of streets or crossing the street
15. Aichmophobia : fear of needles or pointed objects
16. Ailurophobia : fear of cats
17. Albuminurophobia : fear of kidney disease.
18. Alektorophobia : fear of chickens
19. Algophobia : fear of pain
20. Alliumphobia : fear of garlic
21. Allodoxaphobia : fear of opinions
22. Amathophobia : fear of dust
23. Amaxophobia : fear of riding in a car
24. Ambulophobia : fear of walking
25. Amnesiphobia : fear of amnesia
26. Amychophobia : fear of scratches or being scratched
27. Anablephobia : fear of looking up
28. Ancraophobia : fear of wind. (Anemophobia)
29. Androphobia : Abnormal fear of men
30. Anemophobia : fear of air drafts or wind.(Ancraophobia)
31. Anginophobia : fear of angina, choking or narrowness
32. Anglophobia : fear of England or English culture, etc
33. Angrophobia : fear of anger or of becoming angry
34. Ankylophobia : fear of immobility of a joint.
35. Anthrophobia or Anthophobia : fear of flowers

36. Anthropophobia : fear of people or society
37. Antlophobia : fear of floods
38. Anuptaphobia : fear of staying single
39. Apeirophobia : fear of infinity
40. Aphenphosmphobia: fear of being touched (Haphephobia)
41. Apiphobia : fear of bees
42. Apotemnophobia : fear of persons with amputations
43. Arachibutyrophobia: fear of peanut butter sticking to the roof of the mouth
44. Arachnephobia or Arachnophobia : fear of spiders
45. Arithmophobia : fear of numbers
46. Arrhenphobia : fear of men
47. Arsonphobia : fear of fire
48. Asthenophobia : fear of fainting or weakness.
49. Astraphobia : fear of thunder and or Astrapophobia : lightning. (Ceraunophobia, Keraunophobia)
50. Astrophobia : fear of stars or celestial space
51. Asymmetriphobia : fear of asymmetrical things
52. Ataxiophobia : fear of ataxia. (muscular incoordination)
53. Ataxophobia : fear of disorder or untidiness.
54. Atelophobia : fear of imperfection
55. Atephobia : fear of ruin or ruins
56. Athazagoraphobia : fear of being forgotton or ignored or forgetting
57. Atomosophobia : fear of atomic explosions

58. Atychiphobia : fear of failure
59. Aulophobia : fear of flutes
60. Aurophobia : fear of gold
61. Auroraphobia : fear of Northern lights
62. Autodysomophobia : fear of one that has a vile odor.
63. Automatonophobia : fear of ventriloquist's dummies, animatronic creatures, wax statues - anything that falsly represents a sentient being
64. Automysophobia : fear of being dirty
65. Autophobia : fear of being alone or of oneself
66. Aviophobia or Aviatophobia : fear of flying
67. Ballistophobia : fear of missiles
68. Bathophobia : fear of falling from a high place
69. Batophobia : fear of heights or being close to tall buildings
70. Batrachophobia : fear of frogs and toads
71. Belonephobia : fear of pins and needles
72. Bibliophobia : fear of books
73. Blennophobia : fear of slime
74. Brontophobia : fear of thunder and lightning
75. Cancerophobia : fear of cancer
76. Cathisophobia : fear of sitting
77. Cenophobia : fear of empty spaces
78. Chrematophobia : fear of money
79. Cibophobia : fear of or distaste for food
80. Claustrophobia : fear of closed spaces
81. Climacophobia : fear of falling down stairs
82. Clinophobia : fear of staying in bed
83. Cremnophobia : fear of cliffs and precipices
84. Cyberphobia : fear of computers

85. Cynophobia : fear of dogs
86. Dromophobia : fear of crossing streets
87. Dysmorphophobia : fear of physical deformities
88. Ecophobia : fear of home
89. Eleutherophobia : fear of freedom
90. Eosophobia : fear of dawn
91. Ergophobia : fear of work
92. Erotophobia : fear of sex
93. Erythrophobia : fear of red lights or of blushing
94. Euphobia : fear of good news
95. Francophobia : fear of France or the French people
96. Gamophobia : fear of marriage
97. Geniophobia : fear of chins
98. Genophobia : fear of sex
99. Gerascophobia : fear of growing old
100. Graphophobia : fear of writing
101. Gymnophobia : fear of nudity
102. Heliophobia : fear of sunlight
103. Herpetophobia : fear of reptiles
104. Hierophobia : fear of sacred things
105. Homichlophobia : fear of fog
106. Homophobia : fear of homosexuals
107. Hydrophobia : fear of water
108. Hypsophobia : fear of high places
109. Iatrophobia : fear of going to the doctor
110. Iconophobia : fear or hatred of images
111. Kainotophobia : fear of change
112. Kakorrhaphiophobia : fear of failure
113. Kenophobia : fear of empty spaces
114. Ligyrophobia : fear of loud noises
115. Linonophobia : fear of string
116. Lygophobia : fear of darkness

117. Lyssophobia : fear of hydrophobia
118. Macrophobia : fear of prolonged waiting
119. Metrophobia : fear of poetry
120. Monophobia : fear of being alone
121. Muriphobia : fear of mice
122. Mysophobia : fear of contamination or dirt
123. Nebulaphobia : fear of fog
124. Necrophobia : fear of corpses
125. Negrophobia : fear of blacks
126. Neophobia : fear of novelty
127. Nosophobia : fear of disease
128. Novercaphobia : fear of one's stepmother
129. Nyctophobia : fear of the night or darkness
130. Ochlophobia : fear of crowds
131. Oenophobia : fear or hatred of wine
132. Ombrophobia : fear of rain
133. Onomatophobia : fear of hearing a certain word
134. Ophidiophobia : fear of snakes
135. Ophthalmophobia : fear of being stared at
136. Optophobia : fear of opening one's eyes
137. Ornithophobia : fear of birds
138. Paedophobia : fear of children; Fear of dolls
139. Panophobia : Melancholia marked by groundless Fears
140. Pantophobia : fear of everything
141. Parthophobia : fear of virgins
142. Pathophobia : fear of disease
143. Pediculophobia : fear of lice
144. Pentheraphobia : fear or hatred of one's mother-in law
145. Phagophobia : fear of eating
146. Phengophobia : fear of daylight

147.	Phonophobia	:	fear of noise or of speaking aloud
148.	Photophobia	:	fear of light
149.	Pogonophobia	:	fear of beards
150.	Psychrophobia	:	fear of the cold
151.	Pteronophobia	:	fear of being tickled by feathers
152.	Pyrophobia	:	fear of fire
153.	Russophobia	:	fear of Russia or Russians
154.	Satanophobia	:	fear of the devil
155.	Sciaphobia	:	fear of shadows
156.	Scopophobia	:	fear of being looked at by others
157.	Scotophobia	:	fear of the dark
158.	Sitophobia	:	fear of food or eating
159.	Spectrophobia	:	fear of looking in a mirror
160.	Symmetrophobia	:	fear of symmetry
161.	Syphilophobia	:	fear of syphilis
162.	Taphephobia	:	fear of being buried alive
163.	Technophobia	:	fear of technology
164.	Thalassophobia	:	fear of the sea
165.	Thanatophobia	:	fear of death
166.	Theophobia	:	fear of God
167.	Tocophobia	:	fear of pregnancy or childbirth
168.	Tonitrophobia	:	fear of thunder
169.	Topophobia	:	fear of performing; fear of certain places
170.	Toxicophobia	:	fear of poisoning
171.	Triskaidekaphobia	:	fear of the number thirteen
172.	Uranophobia	:	fear of heaven
173.	Xenophobia	:	fear of foreigners
174.	Zelophobia	:	fear of jealousy
175.	Zoophobia	:	fear of animals

□

One-Word That Represents Different Eating Habits

People have interesting and strange eating habits. Some single words are used to denote these peculiar eating habits. A list of such words is mentioned below.

1. Allotriophagy : craving for strange foods
2. Apivorous : eating bees
3. Arachnivorous : feeding on spiders
4. Autocoprophagy : eating one's own feces
5. Autophagy : feeding on body's own tissues
6. Baccivorous : eating berries
7. Batrachivorous : frog-eating
8. Bibliophagist : one who devours books, literally or figuratively
9. Calcivorous : feeding on or living in limestone
10. Cardophagus : donkey; something that eats thistles
11. Carnivorous : one who eats flesh
12. Carpophagous : one who eats fruit
13. Cepivorous : one who eats onion
14. Chthonophagia : one who eats dirt
15. Coprophagous : eating feces

16. Detritivore : animal that eats decomposing organic matter
17. Endophagy : cannibalism within a tribe; eating away from within
18. Entomophagous : eating insects
19. Equivorous : consuming horseflesh
20. Foliophagous : eating leaves; eating folios of books
21. Formivorous : eating ants
22. Fructivorous : feeding on fruit
23. Fucivorous : one who eats seaweed
24. Galactophagist : milk drinker
25. Gamophagia : destruction of one gamete by another
26. Geophagy : practice of feeding on soil; dirt eating
27. Glossophagine : eating using the tongue
28. Graminivorous : feeding on grass or cereals
29. Gumnivorous : feeding on tree saps
30. Herbivorous : eating only plant matter
31. Hippophagy : feeding on horses
32. Homnivorous : eating humans
33. Hylophagous : eating wood
34. Hyperphagia : eating too much
35. Ichthyophagous : fish-eating
36. Insectivorous : plants eating insects
37. Kreatophagia : eating of raw meat
38. Larvivorous : feeding on larvae
39. Lignivorous : feeding on wood
40. Limivorous : eating mud
41. Lithophagous : stone-swallowing; rock-boring; eating rock

42. Lotophagous : feeding on lotuses; indolent; lazy; dreamy
43. Mallophagous : eating wool or fleece
44. Meconophagist : consumer of opium or heroin
45. Meliphagous : feeding upon honey
46. Mellivorous : honey-eating
47. Merdivorous : dung-eating
48. Microphagous : feeding on small creatures or plants
49. Monophagous : feeding on only one type of food
50. Mucivorous : feeding on plant juices
51. Mycophagous : eating fungus
52. Myristicivorous : feeding upon nutmegs
53. Myrmecophagous : feeding on ants
54. Necrophagous : feeding on the dead
55. Nectarivorous : feeding on nectar
56. Nucivorous : nut-eating
57. Omnivorous : eating anything; eating both plant and animal matter
58. Omophagy : eating of raw flesh as a ritual observance
59. Onychophagist : nail-biter
60. Ophiophagous : eating snakes
61. Oryzivorous : rice-eating
62. Ossivorous : feeding on bones
63. Ostreophagous : oyster-eating
64. Ovivorous : eating eggs
65. Paedophage : eater of children
66. Pagophagia : eating trays of ice to help offset iron deficiency
67. Panivorous : bread-eating
68. Pantophagy : omnivorousness

69. Phthirophagous : lice-eating
70. Phyllophagous : leaf-eating
71. Phytivorous : feeding on plants
72. Phytophagous : feeding on vegetable matter
73. Piscivorous : fish-eating
74. Placentophagy : eating of the placenta
75. Plantivorous : plant-eating
76. Plasmophagous : consuming plasma
77. Poephagous : eating grass or herbs; herbivorous
78. Poltophagy : prolonged chewing of food
79. Polyphagous : eating many types of food
80. Psomophagy : swallowing food without thorough chewing
81. Radicivorous : eating roots
82. Ranivorous : eating frogs
83. Rhizophagous : root-eating
84. Rhypophagy : eating filth
85. Sanguivorous : blood-drinking
86. Saprophagous : feeding on decaying material
87. Sarcophagous : feeding on flesh; carnivorous
88. Saurophagous : eating lizards
89. Scatophagous : dung-eating
90. Seminivorous : seed-eating
91. Stercovorous : feeding on dung or excrement
92. Thalerophagous : feeding on fresh vegetable matter
93. Theophagy : sacramental consumption of a god
94. Toxicophagous : eating poisons
95. Univorous : living on only one host or source of food

96. Vegetivorous : eating vegetables
97. Vermivorous : eating worms
98. Xerophagy : eating of dry food; fast of dry food in the week preceding Easter
99. Xylophagous : wood-eating
100. Zoophagy : eating animals

□

Mania Words

There are certain words that have the suffix mania which are one-word substitutes of certain obsessions. Though most of the words are teasing words, some of them are actual words representing excessive obsession. Men are attracted towards certain weird and unusual things. Learn the words

1. Ablutomania : mania for washing oneself
2. Agromania : intense desire to be in open spaces
3. Anglomania : craze or obsession with England and the English
4. Anthomania : obsession with flowers
5. Aphrodisiomania : abnormal sexual interest
6. Arithmomania : obsessive preoccupation with numbers
7. Balletomania : abnormal fondness for ballet
8. Bibliomania : craze for books or reading
9. Bruxomania : compulsion for grinding teeth
10. Cacodemomania : pathological belief that one is inhabited by an evil spirit
11. Catapedamania : obsession with jumping from high places
12. Chinamania : obsession with collecting china

13. Choreomania : dancing mania or frenzy
14. Clinomania : excessive desire to stay in bed
15. Copromania : obsession with feces
16. Dacnomania : obsession with killing
17. Demonomania : pathological belief that one is possessed by demons
18. Dinomania : mania for dancing
19. Dipsomania : abnormal craving for alcohol
20. Discomania : obsession for disco music
21. Doramania : obsession with owning furs
22. Drapetomania : intense desire to run away from home
23. Ecdemomania : abnormal compulsion for wandering
24. Egomania : irrational self-centered attitude or self-worship
25. Eleutheromania : manic desire for freedom
26. Empleomania : mania for holding public office
27. Ergomania : excessive desire to work; workaholism
28. Ethnomania : obsessive devotion to one's own people
29. Eulogomania : obsessive craze for eulogies
30. Flagellomania : abnormal enthusiasm for flogging
31. Francomania : craze or obsession with France and the French
32. Gallomania : craze or obsession with France and the French
33. Gamomania : obsession with issuing odd marriage proposals
34. Graecomania : obsession with Greece and the Greeks

35. Graphomania : obsession with writing
36. Gynaecomania : abnormal sexual obsession with women
37. Habromania : insanity featuring cheerful delusions
38. Hagiomania : mania for sainthood
39. Hellenomania : obsession with Greece and the Greeks; raecomania
40. Hexametromania : mania for writing in hexameter
41. Hieromania : pathological religious visions or delusions
42. Iconomania : obsession with icons or portraits
43. Idolomania : obsession or devotion to idols
44. Infomania : excessive devotion to accumulating facts
45. Kleptomania : irrational predilection for stealing
46. Klopemania : kleptomania
47. Macromania : delusion that objects are larger than natural size
48. Megalomania : abnormal tendency towards grand or grandiose behaviour
49. Melomania : raze for music
50. Methomania : morbid craving for alcohol
51. Micromania : pathological self-deprecation or belief that one is very small
52. Monomania : abnormal obsession with a single thought or idea
53. Morphinomania : habitual craving or desire for morphine
54. Narcomania : uncontrollable craving for narcotics
55. Necromania : sexual obsession with dead bodies; necrophilia

56. Nostomania : abnormal desire to go back to familiar places
57. Nymphomania : excessive or crazed sexual desire
58. Oenomania : obsession or craze for wine
59. Oligomania : obsession with a few thoughts or ideas
60. Oniomania : mania for making purchases
61. Onychotillomania : compulsive picking at the fingernails
62. Orchidomania : abnormal obsession with orchids
63. Parousiamania : obsession with the second coming of Christ
64. Pathomania : moral insanity
65. Peotillomania : abnormal compulsion for pulling on the penis
66. Phaneromania : habit of biting one's nails
67. Pharmacomania : abnormal obsession with trying drugs
68. Phonomania : pathological tendency to murder
69. Photomania : pathological desire for light
70. Planomania : abnormal desire to wander and disobey social norms
71. Polymania : mania affecting several different mental faculties
72. Poriomania : abnormal compulsion to wander
73. Potichomania : craze for imitating oriental porcelain
74. Potomania : abnormal desire to drink alcohol
75. Pseudomania : irrational predilection for lying
76. Rinkomania : obsession with skating
77. Satyromania : abnormally great male sexual desire; satyriasis

78. Sophomania	:	delusion that one is incredibly intelligent
79. Squandermania	:	irrational propensity for spending money wastefully
80. Stampomania	:	obsession with stamp-collecting
81. Syphilomania	:	pathological belief that one is afflicted with syphilis
82. Technomania	:	craze for technology
83. Teutomania	:	obsession with Teutonic or German things
84. Thanatomania	:	belief that one has been affected by death magic, and resulting illness
85. Tomomania	:	irrational predilection for performing surgery
86. Toxicomania	:	morbid craving for poisons
87. Uranomania	:	obsession with the idea of divinity
88. Verbomania	:	craze for words
89. Xenomania	:	inordinate attachment to foreign things
90. Zoomania	:	insane fondness for animals

□

Do It Yourself

Check your knowledge about one-word substitutes. Around 100 questions with four answers are given below. Tick the right one-word substitute for the phrase or sentence given below.

1. A form of government where a few govern the many.
   A. Monarchy B. Oligarchy
   C. Plutocracy D. Autocracy

2. The style in which a writer displays his knowledge.
   A. Pedantic B. Verbose
   C. Pompous D. Ornate

3. The subjects to be considered at a meeting.
   A. Schedule B. Timetable
   C. Agenda D. Plan

4. To leave or remove from a place considered dangerous.
   A. Evade B. Evacuate
   C. Avoid D. Exterminate

5. A person pretending to be somebody he is not.
   A. Magician B. Imposter
   C. Liar D. Rogue

6. Someone who knows many foreign languages.
   A. Linguist B. Grammarian
   C. Polyglot D. Bilingual

7. A person who has little faith in human sincerity and goodness.
   A. Egoist B. Fatalist
   C. Stoic D. Cynic

8. Someone possessing many talents.
   A. Versatile B. Nubile
   C. Exceptional D. Gifted

9. Words inscribed on tomb.
   A. Epitome B. Epistle
   C. Epilogue D. Epitaph

10. The study of ancient societies.
    A. Anthropology B. Archaeology
    C. History D. Ethnology

11. A person who has good understanding, knowledge and reasoning power.
    A. Expert B. Intellectual
    C. Snob D. Literate

12. A person who insists on something.
    A. Disciplinarian B. Stickler
    C. Instantaneous D. Boaster

13. A person or animal that eats every kind of food.
    A. Omnivorous B. Omniscent
    C. Irrestible D. Insolvent

14. Extreme old age when a man behaves like a fool.
    A. Imbecility B. Senility
    C. Dotage D. Superannuation

15. That which cannot be corrected.
    A. Unintelligible B. Indelible
    C. Illegible D. Incorrigible

16. The custom or practice of having more than one husband at the same time.
    A. Polygyny B. Polyphony
    C. Polyandry D. Polychromy

17. A small shop that sells fashionable clothes, cosmetics, etc.
    A. Store B. Stall
    C. Boutique D. Booth

18. That which is unreadable.
    A. Negligible B. Illegible
    C. Ineligible D. Incorrigible

19. In a state of tension or anxiety or suspense.
    A. Off balance B. Depressed
    C. Diffused D. On tenterhooks

20. That which cannot be seen.
    A. Insensible B. Intangible
    C. Invisible D. Unseen

21. Tending to move away from the centre or axis.
    A. Centrifugal B. Centripetal
    C. Axiomatic D. Awry

22. Be the embodiment or perfect example of.
    A. Characterise B. Idol
    C. Personify D. Signify

23. A person who is unsure of the existence of God.
    A. Cynic B. Agnostic
    C. Atheist D. Theist

24. A paper written by hand.
    A. Handicraft B. Manuscript
    C. Handiwork D. Thesis

25. The act of violating the sanctity of the Church is.
    A. Blashphemy B. Heresy
    C. Sacrilege D. Desecration

26. Something that can be heard.
    A. Auditory B. Audio-visual
    C. Audible D. Audition

27. Adopted name of a writer while publishing his writings.
    A. Nickname B. Pseudonym
    C. Nomenclature D. Title

28. Study of birds is called.
    A. Orology B. Optology
    C. Opthalmology D. Ornithology

29. A place that provides refuge.
    A. Asylum B. Sanatorium
    C. Shelter D. Orphanage

30. A child born after death of its father.
    A. Posthumous B. Orphan
    C. Bastard D. Progenitor

31. The absence of law and order.
    A. Rebellion B. Anarchy
    C. Mutiny D. Revolt

32. A Teetotaller means.
    A. One who abstains from theft
    B. One who abstains from meat
    C. One who abstains from taking wine
    D. One who abstains from malice

33. Someone who is interested in collecting, studying and selling of old things.
    A. Antiquarian B. Junk-dealer
    C. Crank D. Archealogist

34. One who is not easily pleased by anything.
    A. Maiden B. Mediaeval
    C. Precarious D. Fastidious

35. A remedy for all diseases.
    A. Stoic B. Marvel
    C. Panacea D. Recompense

36. A person who is fond of fighting.
    A. Bellicose B. Aggressive
    C. Belligerent D. Militant

37. To slap with a flat object.
    A. Chop B. Hew
    C. Gnaw D. Swat

38. A person who is habitually silent.
    A. Serville B. Unequivocal
    C. Taciturn D. Synoptic

39. A person who cannot be corrected.
    A. Incurable B. Incorrigible
    C. Hardened D. Invulnerable

40. A place where bees are kept is called.
    A. An apiary B. A mole
    C. A hive D. A sanctury

41. A religious discourse.
    A. Preach B. Stanza
    C. Sanctorum D. Sermon

42. Parts of a country behind the coast or a river's banks.
    A. Isthumus B. Archipelago
    C. Hinterland D. Swamps

43. The study of the evolution of man as an animal.
    A. Archaeology B. Anthrapology
    C. Chronology D. Ethnology

44. A person who can speak many languages.
    A. Linguist B. Monolingual
    C. Polygot D. Bilingual

45. A person who does not believe in the existence of God.
    A. Egoist B. Atheist
    C. Stoic D. Naïve

46. A disease of mind causing an uncontrollable desire to steal.
    A. Schizophrenia B. Claustrophobia
    C. Kleptomania D. Magolomania

47. A person who scarifies his life for a cause.
    A. Patriot B. Martyr
    C. Revolutionary D. Soldier

48. Someone who brings goods illegally into the country.
    A. Importer B. Exporter
    C. Fraud D. Smuggler

49. To take secretly in small quantities.
    A. Robbery B. Pilferage
    C. Theft D. Defalcation

50. To accustom oneself to a foreign climate.
    A. Adapt B. Adopt
    C. Accustom D. Acclimatise

51. Someone who is all knowledgeable.
    A. Literate B. Scholar
    C. Omnipotent D. Omniscient

52. Detailed plan of journey.
    A. Travelogue B. Travelkit
    C. Schedule D. Itinerary

53. Giving undue favours to one's own kith and kin.
A. Nepotism B. Favouritism
C. Wordliness D. Corruption

54. Hater of learning and knowledge.
A. Misologist B. Bibliophile
C. Misogynist D. Misanthropist

55. A person who is fond of reading books and nothing else.
A. Book-keepr B. Scholar
C. Book-worm D. Student

56. A place where monks live as a secluded community.
A. Cathedral B. Diocese
C. Convent D. Monastery

57. Incapable of being seen through.
A. Ductile B. Opaque
C. Obsolete D. Potable

58. One who does not care for literature or art.
A. Primitive B. Illiterate
C. Philistine D. Barbarian

59. A large sleeping-room with many beds.
A. Bedroom B. Dormitory
C. Hostel D. Basement

60. Continuing fight between parties, families, clans, etc.
A. Enmity B. Feud
C. Quarrel D. Skirmish

61. A building for storing threshed grain.
    A. Hangar B. Dockyard
    C. Store D. Granary

62. Policeman riding on motorcycles as guards to a VIP.
    A. Outriders B. Servants
    C. Commandos D. Attendants

63. One who is determined to exact full vengeance for wrongs done to him.
    A. Virulent B. Vindictive
    C. Usurer D. Vindicator

64. Murder of a king is called.
    A. Infanticide B. Matricide
    C. Genocide D. Regicide

65. An expression of mild disapproval.
    A. Warning B. Denigration
    C. Impertinence D. Reproof

66. One absorbed in his own thoughts and feelings rather than in things outside.
    A. Scholar B. Recluse
    C. Introvert D. Intellectual

67. One who dabbles in fine arts for the love of it and not for monetary gains.
    A. Connoisseur B. Amateur
    C. Professional D. Dilettante

68. A school boy who cuts classes frequently is a.
A. Defeatist B. Sycophant
C. Truant D. Martinet

69. Ready to believe.
A. Credulous B. Credible
C. Creditable D. Incredible

70. Medical study of skin and its diseases.
A. Dermatology B. Endocrinology
C. Gynealogy D. Orthopaedics

71. A person who tries to deceive people by claiming to be able to do wonderful things.
A. Trickster B. Imposter
C. Magician D. Mountebank

72. Someone who believes that all things and events in life are predetermined is a.
A. Fatalist B. Puritan
C. Egoist D. Tyraant

73. Something that relates to everyone in the world.
A. General B. Common
C. Usual D. Universal

74. To walk with slow or regular steps is to.
A. Limp B. Stride
C. Pace D. Advance

75. A style of speaking using too many words.
A. Verbose B. Pedantic
C. Rhetorical D. Abundant

76. Murder of a brother.
A. Patricide B. Regicide
C. Homicide D. Fratricide

77. Having superior or intellectual interests and tastes.
A. Elite B. Highbrow
C. Sophisticated D. Fastidious

78. A dramatic performance.
A. Mask B. Mosque
C. Masque D. Mascot

79. One who does not marry, especially as a religious obligation.
A. Bachelor B. Celibate
C. Vigin D. Recluse

80. That which is perceptible by touch is.
A. Contagious B. Contingent
C. Tenacious D. Tangible

81. Something which is very pleasing to eat.
A. Appetising B. Palatable
C. Tantalising D. Sumptuous

82. The part of government which is concerned with making of rules.
A. Court B. Tribunal
C. Bar D. Legislature

83. To cause troops, etc., to spread out in readiness for battle.
    A. Disperse B. Deploy
    C. Collocate D. Align

84. A loud voice that can be heard by everyone.
    A. Audible B. Applaudable
    C. Laudable D. Oral

85. A light sailing boat built specially for racing.
    A. Canoe B. Yacht
    C. Frigate D. Dinghy

86. A person who looks after a museum.
    A. Curator B. Supervisor
    C. Caretaker D. Warden

87. One who is honourably discharged from service.
    A. Retired B. Emeritius
    C. Relieved D. Emancipated

88. Present opposing arguments or evidence.
    A. Criticise B. Rebuff
    C. Reprimand D. Rebut

89. The policy of extending a country's empire and influence.
    A. Communism B. Internationalism
    C. Capitalism D. Imperialism

90. Of outstanding significance.
    A. Monumental B. Rational
    C. Ominous D. Evident

91. Code of diplomatic etiquette and precedence.
    A. Statesmanship B. Formalism
    C. Hierarchy D. Protocol

92. A fixed orbit in space in relation to earth.
    A. Geological B. Geo-synchronous
    C. Geo-centric D. Geo-stationary

93. That which cannot be believed.
    A. Incredible B. Incredulous
    C. Implausible D. Unreliable

94. To issue a thunderous verbal attack.
    A. Languish B. Animate
    C. Fulminate D. Invigorate

95. A prima facie case is such.
    A. As it seems at first sight
    B. As it is made to seem at first sight
    C. As it turns out to be at the end
    D. As it appear in the beginning

96. As it seems to the court after a number of hearings malafide case is one.
    A. Which is undertaken in a good faith
    B. Which is undertaken in a bad faith
    C. Which is undertaken after a long delay
    D. Which is not undertaken at all

97. The raison d'etre of a controversy is.
    A. The enthusiasm with which it is kept alive
    B. The fitness with which participants handle it
    C. The reason or justification of its existence
    D. The unending hostility the parties concerned have towards each other

98. A place of permanent residence.
   A. Domicile   B. Country
   C. State   D. Owner

99. A masculine woman.
   A. Amazon   B. Spinster
   C. Teenager   D. Widow

100. A prayer Service held at room.
   A. Sext   B. Worship
   C. Pallium   D. Retable

□

Answers

1. (b) Oligarchy
2. (a) Pedantic
3. (c) Agenda
4. (b) Evacuate
5. (d) Rogue
6. (a) Linguist
7. (d) Cynic
8. (a) Versatile
9. (d) Epitaph
10. (b) Archaeology
11. (b) Intellectual
12. (b) Stickler
13. (a) Omnivorous
14. (c) Dotage
15. (d) Incorrigible
16. (c) Polyandry
17. (c) Boutique
18. (b) Ineligible
19. (d) On tenterhooks
20. (c) Invisible
21. (a) Centrifugal
22. (c) Personify

23. (b) Agnostic
24. (b) Manuscript
25. (c) Sacrilege
26. (c) Audible
27. (b) Pseudonym
28. (c) Opthalmology
29. (a) Asylum
30. (a) Posthumous
31. (b) Anarchy
32. (c) One who abstains from taking wine
33. (a) Antiquarian
34. (b) Fastidious
35. (c) Panacea
36. (a) Bellicose
37. (d) Swat
38. (c) Taciturn
39. (c) Hardened
40. (a) An apiary
41. (d) Sermon
42. (c) Hinterland
43. (b) Anthrapology
44. (c) Polygot
45. (b) Atheist
46. (c) Kleptomania
47. (b) Martyr
48. (d) Smuggler
49. (b) Pilferage
50. (d) Acclimatise
51. (d) Omniscient
52. (d) Itinerary
53. (a) Nepotism
54. (a) Misologist

55. (c) Book-worm
56. (c) Convent
57. (b) Opaque
58. (c) Philistine
59. (b) Dormitory
60. (b) Feud
61. (d) Granary
62. (a) Outriders
63. (b) Vindictive
64. (d) Regicide
65. (d) Reproof
66. (c) Introvert
67. (b) Amateur
68. (c) Truant
69. (a) Credulous
70. (a) Dermatology
71. (a) Trickster
72. (a) Fatalist
73. (d) Universal
74. (c) Pace
75. (a) Verbose
76. (d) Fratricide
77. (b) Highbrow
78. (c) Masque
79. (c) Celibate
80. (d) Tangible
81. (b) Palatable
82. (d) Legislature
83. (b) Deploy
84. (a) Audible
85. (b) Yacht
86. (a) Curator

87. (a) Retired
88. (d) Rebuff
89. (d) Imperialism
90. (a) Monumental
91. (d) Protocol
92. (d) Geo-stationary
93. (a) Incredible
94. (c) Fulminate
95. (a) As it seems at first sight
96. (b) Which is undertaken in a bad faith
97. (c) The reason or justification of its existence
98. (a) Domicile
99. (a) Amazon
100. (a) Sext

□□□